THE PARSEES

THE PARSEES:

THEIR HISTORY, MANNERS, CUSTOMS, AND RELIGION.

BY

DOSABHOY FRAMJEE

GYAN

Published by

Gyan Publishing House
5, Ansari Road
Daryaganj, New Delhi-110002
Phone: 011-47034999, 9811692060
E-mail: books@gyanbooks.com

Distribution Network
gyanbooks.com
India, USA, Canada, UK, Australia, France

ISBN : 978-81-212-3877-9 (PB)
First Published, 1858

2nd Impression 2020

Printed at: Gyan Press, Delhi.

The Parsees
Author: Dosabhoy Framjee

THE PARSEES:

THEIR HISTORY, MANNERS, CUSTOMS, AND RELIGION.

BY

DOSABHOY FRAMJEE.

LONDON:
SMITH, ELDER AND CO., 65, CORNHILL.
BOMBAY: SMITH, TAYLOR AND CO.

1858.

TO THE

PARSEES OF WESTERN INDIA

This Record

OF

THEIR HISTORY, MANNERS, CUSTOMS, AND RELIGION,

IS AFFECTIONATELY DEDICATED

BY

DOSABHOY FRAMJEE.

PREFACE.

THE vast empiro known in Europe as thc "East Indics" holds a population of onc hundred and eighty millions of persons, thc bulk of whom arc either followers of Mahomcd or professors of Hindooism. Scatterod over the continent, but especially in Bombay, another racc is, however, to be mct with, differing essentially from both Mahomedans and Hindoos. The members composing this raec arc known as Parsees, and are the descendants of the ancient Persians who emigrated to India on the conquest of their country by the Arabs. Compared with thc number of the other natives of India, the Parsees add so insignificant a quota to thc population, that their existence to very many Europeans is not even known, while those who are aware that such a race exists very often confound them with the Hindoos and Mahomedans.

The object of the present work is to make the English public acquainted with the history, belief, and manners of the Parsees, who, though unimportant in point of numbers, have, by their commercial habits, formed an important link between the English in India and the native inhabitants. Throughout the rebellion in the East the Parsees have maintained an unshaken loyalty to the British, whom they are proud to call their fellow-subjects, and while preserving their own independence of religion and customs, their chief desire is that the British rule in India should be consolidated upon a basis of strict justice and mutual interest.

A perusal of the following pages will show that the Parsees are a distinct race, and that neither in their religion nor in their habits of life, do they assimilate with either the Mahomedans or the Hindoos. The Parsees are endeavouring to follow the example which the British have set them. Western civilization has had great influence on their characters, and they are now eagerly embracing the opportunities for improvement and advancement that are offered to them. When the distinguishing characteristics of the people of Oriental nations are taken into consideration, it must be evident that the Parsees form a striking exception to the other races, and on this account the author feels less diffidence in bringing the history of his people under the notice of the British public.

The author is desirous that his European readers should bear in mind, that the present work is the production of a foreigner, in whose writing any errors of composition may be pardoned, as arising from the circumstances of his birth and position: the want of an idiomatic knowledge of the language in which he writes, may have deprived his pages of all grace of style. He is conscious, however, that he has most rigidly adhered to truth, and should he have succeeded in rendering his narrative clear and intelligible, the object with which he set out will have been fully accomplished.

London, July 23rd, 1858.

CONTENTS.

CHAPTER V.

COMMERCIAL PURSUITS.

CHAPTER VI.

EDUCATION.

CHAPTER VII.

RELIGION.

CHAPTER VIII.

CONCLUSION.

THE PARSEES,

THEIR

HISTORY, MANNERS, CUSTOMS, AND RELIGION.

CHAPTER I.

HISTORICAL SKETCH.

The Parsees, the Descendants of the Ancient Persians—Overthrow of the Ancient Persian Monarchy by the Arabs—Character of the Mahomedan Conquerors—Conversion of the Zoroastrians to Mahomedanism—Their retreat into Khorasan.—Emigration to Ormus—Voyage to India—Arrival at Diew—Removal to Sanjan—Interview with the Rajah—Terms of landing—Building of a Fire Temple—Emigration to different Cities of Guzrat—Fight with the Mahomedan Army of the Sultan of Ahmedabad—Ultimate Defeat of the Hindoo Rajah—Conquest of Sanjan by the Mahomedans—The Parsees quit Sanjan.—Their Opposition to the Troops of the Rajah at Ruttonpoor—Massacre of the Parsees at Variao—Improvement of their Condition at Surat and Nowsaree—Arrival at Bombay—Invasion of Bombay by the Hubshis of Junjeera.—Their Expulsion—Services of Dorabjee Nanabhoy.

THE remnant of that mighty and flourishing race of people who inhabited Persia centuries before the Christian era, and whose dominion, in its most prosperous period, reached as far as the Persian Gulf and Indian Ocean on the south, the rivers Indus and Oxus on the east, the Caspian Sea and Caucasian Mountains on the north, and the deserts of Lybia and the Mediterranean on the west, whose grandeur, magnificence, and glory were unequalled by any nation of ancient times; whose kings were at once the most powerful of monarchs, and the wisest and most beneficent of rulers; that remnant is known in India under the designation of Parsees, a name which they derive from their original country, Pars or Fars. That province, called by the Greeks, Persis, contained the chief city of the empire, and the most splendid of the royal palaces, and from it the whole kingdom gained its name. Of the remnant of the ancient Persians now found in Western India, and chiefly in Bombay, where they form a most numerous and respectable class of the population, it is proposed to give in this publication a short history.

The difficulties which beset the fulfilment of such a task are many. Isolated accounts of the exodus of the Parsees from Persia, under the pressure of Mahomedan invasion, and of their arrival on the shores of India; of their manners, customs and religion, are to be met with in the pages of learned Orientalists, where they are inaccessible to the general reader, while fragmentary notices of the race are to be found in the records of the historian and the jottings of travellers. But a connected narrative of this people, who, though unimportant in point of numbers, have earned a distinguished name for themselves in India by industry and commercial enterprise, and by closely identifying themselves with the interests of the supreme power in the country, has not yet been laid before the English public. To supply, in some measure, this desideratum is the object of the present work.

To enter upon the history of the ancient Persians, the ancestors of the Parsees, would be foreign to the subject; the public have already been put in possession of all the facts that are, or probably can be, known concerning them. Suffice it to say, that with Yezdézird, the forty-fifth king in the descent of the race of Kaimurs, ended the ancient Persian monarchy. The neighbouring and wealthy empire of Persia presented too tempting a prize to the fanatic and ambitious spirit, evoked by Mahomed, to remain long unmolested, and in the middle of the seventh century of the Christian era, the Arab sword invaded Persia, under Caliph Omar. In a fierce and well-contested battle with the Persians at the village of Náhávánd, about fifty miles from the ancient city of Ecbatana, the fate of the empire was decided. The Persian army, numbering fifteen thousand fighting men, was defeated with great slaughter. Yezdézird, abandoning his kingdom as lost, fled the country; and, after wandering in solitude and disguise for a period of ten years, was at last treacherously slain by a miller, to whom the secret of his identity had been confided.* This event occurred A.D. 651, and thus ended the dynasty of the Sussanian Kings of Persia, and the monarchy founded by Kaikhoshru, the Cyrus the Great of the Greeks. With the overthrow of the monarchy every vestige of Persian magnificence disappeared, and the empire with its glories, became the inheritance of the Mahomedans, whose supremacy in the newly conquered kingdom was at once established.

History has faithfully drawn the character of the Mahomedan conquerors wherever they have appeared, and has traced their footsteps in characters of blood. Toleration in religion

* Owing to this circumstance, "a miller's trust" has passed into a proverb in Persia.

is unknown to the haughty, uncivilized barbarian believers in the Koran. Bigotry is the highest virtue demanded of the Mahomedan, and one which secures for him favour in the eyes of his prophet and his God, and takes him by the shortest route to a place in heaven. Thus on the conquest of Persia, the Mahomedan soldiers of the Caliphat of Bagdad traversed the length and breadth of the country, presenting the alternative of death or the Koran, and compelling the conquered nation to accept the one or the other. By these oppressive and cruel means, a hundred thousand persons are said to have daily abjured the faith of their forefathers; and the fire-temples and other sacred places were destroyed or converted into mosques. Under such rulers, almost the whole Zoroastrian population of Persia embraced the faith of Islam, and nearly every trace of the religion of Zoroaster was obliterated.

Historians have noted that the effect of the Mahomedan conquest (for to call it conversion would be simply ridiculous) was greatly demoralizing to the people. The ancient Greeks have borne testimony to the character for truth of their Persian contemporaries, while modern writers have denounced the Persians of our own times as a nation of liars. Such of the followers of Zoroaster as preferred obeying the dictates of their conscience, to freeing themselves from the persecution of their rulers by accepting the Koran, abandoned their homes, and fled to the mountainous districts of Khorassan, where for a time they succeeded in evading the pursuit of their terrible foe. For about a hundred years they remained in Khorassan in the unmolested enjoyment and practice of their religion. But persecution at last reached them even in those remote districts, and they were once more compelled to fly from the enemies of their faith, and a considerable number emigrated to the little island of Ormus, at the mouth of the Persian Gulf.

Their stay at this retreat was, however, but of short duration. They were yet within the reach of their cruel persecutors, and rather than fall into the hands of the fanatic, impious *devs* (devils) they at last determined to relinquish for ever the land of their forefathers, and to remove to a country where they might hope to live in tranquillity, and in the enjoyment of their social and religious rights. Acting upon this determination, they sought an asylum in the country of the

Hindoos, and are said to have engaged at Ormus several vessels for their transport, and placing their wives and children on board they set sail towards the distant shores of India.* It is impossible to suppose that this was the only exodus of the Persians from the land of their fathers. That several emigrations took place at successive periods, as the flame of the fanatic zeal and persecuting spirit of the Mahomedans burned more or less brightly, can hardly be doubted. Various meagre and unsatisfactory traditions exist concerning the tide of emigration, the manner in which it was effected, and the total number of those who left the shores of the Gulf. Whatever information is now in our possession, and is to any extent reliable, is gleaned from a work entitled Kissah-i-Sanjan, which was compiled in the year 1599, by one Behram a Zoroastrian resident of Nowsaree†, from the traditions extant in his time. According to that writer, the first port in Hindostan at which the earliest refugees arrived was Div

* That intercourse of some sort or other had previously existed between the ancient Persians and Hindoos has been satisfactorily proved. Some of the latter, who were famed for wisdom and learning, had made Persia their residence for many years.

† A town situated about twenty miles south of Surat.

or Diew*, a small island in the Gulf of Cambay, lying to the south-west of the peninsula of Kattiwar. Here it is said they disembarked and took up their residence for nineteen years, at the expiration of which period they quitted Diew to find another place of adoption. The causes which led to this migration have not been satisfactorily explained; but the following mysterious passage relating to the event is to be found in Behram's work:—"An aged Dastoor (high priest) reading the tablets of the stars, made an augury that it behoved them to depart from that place, and seek out another abode. All rejoiced at his words, and sailed swiftly towards Guzrat."

That misfortunes never come singly was literally fulfilled in the case of this outcast

* "Div or Diew was one of the earliest seats of the Portuguese power in India. It was regarded by Albuquerque as an excellent port for a settlement, one that would secure, from its advantages, both marine and terrene, the permanency of the country's influence in Hindostan. After several fruitless efforts, the infamous Nugna d'Acunha succeeded, in 1535, in obtaining possession of Diew, and within a very short time rendered it almost impregnable to the assaults of the native powers. . . . History asserts that the trade of Surat was destroyed to encourage commerce at Diew; and Osorio makes mention of the splendour of its buildings and the greatness of its maritime powers. Upon Surat recovering itself, Diew declined, and is now said to be a vast pile of dilapidation."—*Brigg's Cities of Guzarástra.*

people, for hardly had they lost sight of land when a severe storm overtook the little fleet, and deprived them of all hope. Rather than abandon the faith they had inherited from their fathers, they had voluntarily made themselves exiles for ever from the land that gave them birth, and were now at the mercy of strangers for a home, and now at the mercy of the treacherous deep in seeking more friendly shores. What wonder then that the little band, confused and in despair, were ready to believe that they were the sport of merciless fate. But, though sick at heart, their better sense does not seem to have entirely forsaken them. In their helplessness they called to mind Him who is the author of all good, the Preserver, Supporter and Cherisher of the poor and the distressed, and who never fails to listen to the supplications of the humble and meek.

To rescue them from the impending danger, they are said to have offered up the following prayer to the throne of the Most High. "O wise God, come to our assistance in this jeopardy; and we pray to Thee to deliver us from the impending danger. O glorious God, we beseech Thee to gladden our hearts by removing these difficulties with which we are now surrounded. On Thy goodness, O Lord, we fully depend, and hope that the storm which has overtaken us will soon be over through Thy Divine Grace. As long as we have hopes of Thy aid, O God, we tremble not at this calamity. We have implicit faith in Thee, as the hearer of those who cry to Thee. Deliver us, therefore, O Merciful Providence, from this trouble, and lead us to the right path, that we may escape from this sea to the shores of India, and we promise, O Lord, to kindle on high the flame sacred to Thee in grateful remembrance of thy kindness and protection."

We may suppose that their prayer was heard, for the storm abated and a gentler gale carried them in safety to Sanjan about twenty-five miles south of Damaun, where they landed about the year A.D. 717. The territory of Sanjan was then under the rule of a wise and liberal chief named Jadao Rana. A Dastoor or high priest of the Parsees was accordingly sent to the Rana with fitting presents, in order to obtain from him the terms of their landing. The Dastoor, a venerable old man, on approaching the Rana blessed him, and having explained the reasons which caused the Parsees to relinquish their native country, and detailed their vicissitudes and sufferings, requested to be allowed to reside in the city of Sanjan. It is said, that the Prince, struck with the warlike and hardy appearance of the men who came as refugees to his court, had some fear for the safety of his throne and country, and before granting the desired permission requested the chief priest to explain to him the secret of their affairs and the nature of their faith.

During their stay at Diew, the Parsees acquired a knowledge of the language, religion, manners and customs of the Hindoos, and were enabled to answer the inquiries of the Rajah so satisfactorily that no opposition was made by him to their making Sanjan their place of abode and their adopted country. The learned among the Parsees prepared sixteen *schlokes* or distiches, and in these they briefly described the tenets of their religion and their mode of worship. As it will doubtless interest the European reader to know what those *schlokes* contained, they are given entire, though they must not be supposed to give a complete abstract of the Parsee faith.

1st. We are worshippers of Hormuzd (Supreme Being) and the sun and five elements.

2nd. We observe silence while bathing, praying, making offerings to fire, and eating.

3rd. We use incense, perfumes, and flowers in our religious ceremonies.

4th. We are worshippers of the cow.

5th. We wear the sacred garment, the *sadrâ* or shirt, the *kusti* or cincture for the loins and the cap of two folds.

6th. We rejoice in songs and instruments of music on the occasion of our marriages.

7th. We ornament and perfume our wives.

8th. We are enjoined to be liberal in our charities, and especially in excavating tanks and wells.

9th. We are enjoined to extend our sympathies towards males as well as females.

10th. We practise ablutions with *gaomutra*, one of the products of the cow.

11th. We wear the sacred girdle when praying and eating.

12th. We feed the sacred flame with incense.

13th. We practise devotion five times a day.

14th. We are careful observers of conjugal fidelity and purity.

15th. We perform annual religious ceremonies on behalf of our ancestors.

16th. We place great restraints on our women after their confinements.

The reader is here cautioned against supposing the foregoing to be the fundamental principles of the Parsee religion. The Parsees are not the idolatrous people which the preceding dogmas would lead one to suppose, and ample opportunity will be given to the reader of forming an opinion as to the true religion of the Parsees in subsequent pages of this work. It is necessary here to state frankly, that the first refugees of our faith in India played the part of dissemblers and that the distiches appear to have been framed with the view of gaining the favour of the Hindoo Rajah. While allusion is made therein to many minor ceremonies, which are no more the essentials of Zoroastrianism than of Christianity, yet because of their approximating to certain ceremonies of the Hindoos, prominence is given to them, while silence is preserved regarding those doctrines on which the religion of Zoroaster is really based.

The Parsee refugees had sufficient opportunities of learning at Diew, how jealous the Hindoos are of association with people of other castes, from the dread of contamination fatal to themselves. Followed as they had been by continual misfortunes, and cast upon the world without country or home; the Parsees could not but be anxious to obtain, even at a great sacrifice, a landing place for themselves and their families. Bearing this in view, it is possible that they answered the inquiries of the Hindoo Rajah in such a form as to win his good opinion. They concealed from the Prince all that would have appeared extraordinary or offensive to him and his subjects, and supplied, in place thereof, ceremonies which had an origin exclusively Hindoo.

The device succeeded; and the people found favour in Jadao Rana's eyes, and permission was given them to reside in his city, on condition of their adopting the language of the country, and ceasing to speak that of their forefathers. They were also required to dress their females in the Indian fashion, to wear no armour, and to perform the marriage ceremonies of their children at night, in conformity with the practice of the Hindoos. The exiles had but two alternatives—to accept these conditions, or to return to their ships; and rather than become once more wanderers on the face of the earth, they chose the former course, and rested in the land of the Rajah. On being directed to occupy any vacant ground they pleased, they selected a large tract of waste land in the immediate vicinity of Sanjan.

After a long series of hardships endured for many years, the exiles had at last found a resting place, and might expect repose and happiness. Every one now betook himself to his profession, and their settlement which, but a short time before, was a sterile desert, became converted into a populous and thriving city. Neither did the Parsees forget Him who had assisted them in their day of trouble. They remembered the vow which they had made to "kindle on high the flame sacred to Him," in grateful memory of their deliverance from the hand of death, and they embraced the earliest opportunity of intimating to the Rajah their intention of building, with his permission, a fire-temple in Sanjan, in fulfilment of the solemn vow which they had made. As the Hindoos themselves hold fire in veneration, not only was the desired permission at once accorded, but every assistance was rendered to further the object. The fire-temple was, however, wholly and exclusively constructed by the Parsees themselves, the Rajah merely supplying various articles which would expedite the great work. A few years witnessed the completion of the temple (A.D. 721), and saw the sacred fire kindled on its altar in accordance with the rights of the Zoroastrian religion.

For about three hundred years after their landing in Sanjan, the Parsees are said to have lived in peace and quietness. At the end of that period their number was greatly increased. Many of them had emigrated with their families to Surat, Nowsari, Broach, Variao, Ukleser and Cambay,* places now easily recognised on the map of Guzerat. Two hundred years more rolled on and no records are left of the Parsees that are worth noting beyond the fact that they chiefly occupied themselves wherever they were located in agricultural pursuits. They seem ever to have lived amicably with the Hindoos; for during this long period of five centuries there is no tradition of any misunderstanding between the strangers and the children of the soil.

About the year A.D 1507, the Parsees of Sanjan are said to have greatly distinguished themselves by their valor in assisting their

* Some accounts state that direct emigration from Persia also took place to these cities long after the landing of the first colony at Sanjan.

Raja against the aggression of a Mahomedan chief, Sultan Mahomed Begada, who was residing at Ahmedabad. This chief was surnamed Begada from his having conquered the two hill forts of Joonagud and Champanir. While at the latter place, he formed a design for subverting the independence of Sanjan, and soon after collected a large army under a skilful general named Aluf Khan to effect this object.

The Mahomedan general, with thirty thousand men, arrived before Sanjan, and the Hindoo monarch, conscious of the insufficiency of his resources to cope with the hardy soldiers of the enemy trembled for his crown and country. He solicited the assistance of the Parsees, and summoning them to his presence addressed them as follows:—"My ancestors exalted you and lavished favours upon your people, and it behoves you in this my difficulty to show your gratitude, and to exert yourself on my behalf, and lead the way in battle." The Parsees were not unmindful of their obligations to the former rulers of Sanjan and at once undertook to defend the country which had so hospitably welcomed their forefathers to its shores. To the address of the Rajah they replied. "Fear not, O Prince, on account of this army: all of us are ready to scatter the heads of thy foes and will fight as long as a drop of blood remains in our veins. In battle we never give way; not one man of us will turn his back though a millstone were dashed at his head."

In adopting this resolve the Parsees were not unmindful of the persecutions sustained by their ancestors, and they determined that the Mahomedan invaders should be repelled at any sacrifice. The cause of the Hindoo monarch was their own; they knew that if the army of the Sultan was successful their religion would again be perilled, and a second persecution of their faith instituted. Notwithstanding the oath they had taken never to bear arms, they considered that in this extremity they were fully justified in drawing the sword to defend the territories of the Hindoo Rajah, and a force of fourteen hundred Zoroastrians, under the leadership of one Ardeshir was immediately added to the Hindoo army.

This accession to his force caused the Raja to take courage; every preparation was made for the impending struggle, which was to decide the fate of his kingdom, and a fierce battle is said to have ensued, a few miles beyond

Sanjan. Sword, javelin, and arrow did their leadly work, and many fell on both sides. In he thick of the battle the Hindoos were unable to keep their ground against the urious onslaught of the Mahomedans, and led the field. The noble band of Persian llies, however, was not dismayed. They vere fighting for their faith and for their homes, and the interests involved in the issue of the contest made them regardless of their ives. Their brave leader, Ardeshir, heroically ed them on, and attacking the enemy furiously, roke their ranks, and threw them into confusion. The whole force was discomfited, and Aleef Khan fled, leaving Ardeshir and his ittle band masters of the field.

The Mahomedan armies in India have generally been successful over those of the Hindoos, from the hardy and warlike character of their soldiers. This defeat of thousands f their number, which was rendered more humiliating, from the fact of its having been aused by a handful of strangers, was more han their proud spirits could endure. Aluf Khan raised reinforcements, and again appeared in the field. Ardeshir emboldened by uccess was not, however, to be daunted, and he ddressed the Hindoo Rajah in the following spirited terms. "Oh, Prince, the enemy has appeared in greater numbers than before. They are a hundred to our one, but behold our courage. We will either yield our lives, or take those of our foes, and in this resolve may God befriend us, since he always removes our difficulties."

In the battle that followed, Ardeshir was engaged in single combat with a Mahomedan chief of note. The gallant Parsee general hurled him from his horse, and killed him with his sword. Aluf Khan, it is said, witnessing the scene became furiously excited, and led on in person a heavy charge against the Parsees. The two armies joined in battle, and blood flowed in torrents. Fortune did not favour the allies on this occasion. A dart struck the Parsee leader, who fell headlong from his saddle, and as is the case with all Oriental nations, the army having lost its chief hesitated and gave way, and was completely routed by the enemy. The Hindoo prince is also said to have fallen in this battle. Aluf Khan was now master of Sanjan, and the Parsees soon found it impossible to call that place any longer their home.

After the overthrow of the Hindoo Government the Parsees suffered many wrongs at the hands of the Mahomedan troops, and the greater part of them fled to the mountains of Baharout, taking with them the sacred fire which they had consecrated at Sanjan.* For twelve years they sojourned in these mountains, and then directed their course to a place called Bansda, where a small colony of Parsees existed at the time. The sacred fire was also carried thither, and after some years it was removed to Nowsaree where the Parsees had become an influential and opulent race. In late years, owing to some disputes among the priests, it was secretly removed to Oodwara thirty-two miles south of Surat, where it still exists, and being the oldest fire temple of the Zoroastrians in India, is held in the highest veneration.

Nothing worth chronicling is known of the history of the Parsees who before the overthrow of the Hindoo Rajah of Sanjan emigrated to different cities of Guzrat.

The emigrants wherever they located themselves pursued the quiet and peaceful arts of husbandry. But their national energy and

* Not a single Parsee is to be found at Sanjan at the present day, and the ruins of a *dokhma*, or "tower of silence," for the dead, is now the only memento that exists of the Parsees' settlement in that place.

courage never seem to have forsaken them; in proof of which an affair at Variao may be cited. A small Parsee colony had settled at that place, which is situated at some distance from Surat, and was at the time under the rule of the Raja of Ruttonpore, a Rajpoot chief. This chief attempted to extort an extraordinary tribute from these Parsees, and the latter, refusing to submit to the extortion, opposed and defeated the troops sent to enforce the claim.

Unable to revenge themselves openly, the soldiers of the Rajah sought an opportunity of surprising those who had defeated them in the field, and a marriage festival, to which all the Parsees in the place were invited, was seized as the occasion for gratifying their cowardly revenge. Unconscious of what was impending, the Parsees were surprised in the midst of their festivities, and with the women and children were ruthlessly murdered by the ruffians. The anniversary of this cruel tragedy perpetrated upon the Parsees at Variao is still kept at Surat, and religious ceremonies are performed on the occasion in honour of those who fell on that melancholy day.

Though the Parsees lived in tranquillity and in the full enjoyment of their religious rights under the government of the Hindoo Rajahs of Sanjan none of them made any advance towards the acquirement of wealth or influence until after they abandoned that territory. Their dispersion appears to have been the signal for their attaining prosperity in Surat and Nowsaree. Considering the relations existing between the Parsees and the Mahomedans, it is strange to find that they secured the favour of the Nawabs of the former city, and were by them entrusted with minor offices in the state.

Nek Saut Khan, the ancestor of the well-known Ardeshir Dhunjeesha of Surat, had gained considerable approbation and honours at the hands of the great Mogul himself. Owing to his skill and knowledge in mechanics, he was sent by the Nawab of Surat to the Court of Agra, where the Mogul was so much delighted with his diligence, that a Jageer in the Zilla of Surat was bestowed upon him in perpetuity. It is well known that through the medium of his great interest, some valuable privileges were obtained for the English at Surat about the middle of the eighteenth century.

Parsee tradition says, that there lived in the middle of the sixteenth century at Nowsaree, a Zoroastrian named Maneksha, who was reputed to be very wealthy and who maintained a princely state. About this time or a little later, the Parsees succeeded at Surat in acquiring wealth and influence, but their importance at that station rose considerably after the establishment of the European factories there. Their energy, industry, and peculiar customs made so wide a distinction between them and the other natives of India, as to gain the notice of the Dutch and other European settlers. They carried on business as brokers to European firms, and through them goods were bought and sold, a position which the Parsees hold to the present day in most of the European firms in Bombay.

Muncherjee Seth, whose influence with the Nawab of Surat was very great, and whose name at present is deeply venerated by the Parsees, was broker to the Dutch factory at Surat. In fact, the Parsees were almost the sole channel of intercourse, between the Europeans and the natives of Surat. This city, even in its present decayed state, affords conclusive evidence of the opulence and wealth of the Parsees of former days. As Surat rose in importance, Nowsaree sank into insignificance. The latter place is now only known as the city of the Parsee priests, numbers of whom are every year sent to Bombay to minister to the spiritual wants of the Parsee population of that city.

No authentic records exist to show the exact date of the arrival of the Parsees in Bombay, nor to explain what was the motive that led them thither. Probably the English merchants of Surat induced some of them to settle in Bombay for the purposes of trade. This much may safely be affirmed, that their first settlement in that island was a little before or about the time when it was ceded to the British by the Crown of Portugal, as the dowry of Catherine, Princess of Portugal, who became the wife of Charles the Second of England, A.D. 1668.

Dr. Fryer, who visited Bombay in the year 1671, says:—"On the other side of the great inlet to the sea is a great point abutting against Old Woman's Island, and is called Malabar Hill, a rocky woody mountain, yet sends forth long grass; *on the top of all is a Parsee tomb lately raised.*" The first work of the Parsees wherever they settle, is to construct a tomb (*dokhma*) or tower of silence for the reception of their dead, and the statement of Dr. Fryer that the tomb in question had been recently raised, is a sufficient proof that no considerable number of the Parsees could have settled in that island, prior to its cession to the British.

So far as we have been able to ascertain from tradition among the Parsees themselves, Dorabjee Nanabhoy was the first and only individual of the race, who resided with his family in Bombay when the island was under the sway of the Portuguese Goverment. He was employed by the authorities in transacting miscellaneous business with the natives of the place. When the island was ceded to England, he was appointed to a similar office; and, as the new rulers were ignorant of the place, manners, language, and customs of the people, he was frequently consulted by them on affairs of state.* We may also infer

*Some notice of the services rendered by the descendants of Dorabjee Nanabhoy to the Bombay government in its early stages is required at our hands. In 1692 a severe plague broke out in Bombay, when most of the Europeans of the place and soldiers in the garrison fell victims to the disease. Taking advantage of this unfortunate circumstance, the Seedees of Jungeera, who were then a powerful and independent people, invaded Bombay with a large force, and took possession of the island and Dungerry fort (now called Fort George). Dorabjee's son Rustom Dorab, who had succeeded his father in the service of the Bombay government, undertook to drive away the Seedees from the place. He raised a militia from among the fishermen of the population, fought the invaders and defeated them. He then despatched messengers with the news of the victory to the chief of the English factory at Surat, who soon after arrived in Bombay and took charge of the government. For these invaluable services Rustom Dorab was honored, with the hereditary title

that at the time of Dr. Fryer's visit to Bombay, the number of Parsees living there must have been very insignificant, as that gentleman makes no mention of them in the description given by him of the inhabitants then comprising the population of the island.

Another early Parsee settler at Bombay was one Lowjee a shipwright. He left Surat, his native city, for Bombay, at the advice of a Mr. Dudley, who superintended the building of the East India Company's vessels at the former place. His attainments in the art of ship-building were of no inferior

of Patel (lord or chief) of Bombay. He was also placed at the head of the fisherman caste, and invested with the authority of adjudicating civil and religious disputes among them, an authority which, up to this day, is enjoyed by his descendants. On the death of Rustom Dorab, his son Cowasjee Rustomjee was invested with a dress of honour by Governor Hornby. As in those days the Government found much difficulty in providing tonnage for transporting troops from one place to another, Cowasjee Patel was entrusted with the provision of boats and tonnage for the public service, which duty he performed very creditably. When the British took Tannah from the Mahrattas, Cowasjee Patel was appointed to an important post in the place, where he colonized a number of Parsees, and built places of worship and other charitable buildings for their use from his own purse. On the death of Cowasjee his son, Sorabjee, succeeded to the title of "Patel." The present head of this family, Hirjeebhoy Rustomjee Cowasjee Patel, was until lately one of the most extensive merchants in China and is at present in England.

order, and his search after employment and fortune seems to have been attended with the most favourable results. Under his supervision the Bombay Dockyard was founded in the year 1735, and it is worthy of remark that the post of master builder in this factory has ever since been filled by descendants of Lowjee. After Lowjee, the other notable arrivals in Bombay, were those of the *Shet Khandan*, the *Dadyshet*, and the *Banajee* families. Descendants of all these families still survive and enjoy honourable positions among the Parsees of Bombay. That enlightened and eminent man the late Framjee Cowasjee, whose name is known all over India, belonged to the Banajee family. The Dadyshets are still extensively engaged in trade, and the Shet Khandans is a wealthy retired family.

We have thus brought down our history to the arrival of the Parsees in Bombay. Their rise and progress in this island is described in subsequent pages. In the chapter immediately succeeding, it is proposed to inquire into the state of such of the Zoroastrians, as are still to be met with in their native country.

CHAPTER II.

THE PARSEES IN PERSIA.

Effect of Mahomedan invasion on the country and natives of Persia—Zoroastrian population at Yezd and Kirman—Their occupation—Causes which led to their destruction—Invasion of Persia by the Gilji Afghans—Persecutions to which the Parsees were subjected by the invaders—Persecution under Lootf Ally Khan—Enlistment of the Zoroastrians in the Ranks of the Afghan Troops—Their further persecutions in the reign of Nadir Shah and of Aga Mahomed Khan Kujur—Condition of the Zoroastrians at Yezd and Kirman—Measures taken by the Parsees of Bombay for the improvement of the condition of their coreligionists in Persia—Miseries and hardships of the capitation tax—Treatment of the Zoroastrians by the other subjects of Persia—Impediment to their pursuit of commerce—Difficulty in recovering their claims—Extraordinary instances of oppression and injustice—Physical and Moral Condition of the Zoroastrians of Persia—The means by which their miseries might be alleviated—Contrast of British and Persian rule as manifested in the condition of the Parsees of Persia and those of India.

An inquiry into the present state of the professors of Zoroastrianism would manifestly be incomplete if it did not embrace an account of such of the race as have held fast that profession in the mother country, ever since its conquest, by the Moslem invaders. The effect of Mahomedan rule, wherever it has been established, is too well known to need any lengthened description here. Within a hundred years of the time when the followers of the Arabian prophet first set foot on the Persian soil, the condition and circumstances of the country were entirely changed. Lands once fertile, had become dreary wastes, and the fields where the golden corn waved were deserted by the husbandman, and became the pasture ground of wild animals; the ploughshares were beaten into swords, and the pruning hooks into spears. The country, once the home of peace and plenty, was everywhere thrown into confusion, while hordes of robbers, driven into crime by the distresses of the times, traversed every part of the land perpetrating the most cruel atrocities.

Persia once fallen never revived, but gradually sank into its present insignificance. Perhaps no country in the world, has witnessed so many revolutions as that unhappy land, the tyrants who filled the throne, commonly owed their elevation to treachery and blood. The professors of nearly every religion, but that of Islam, have endured constant persecution, while the treatment experienced by the inhabitants of the ancient faith of Zoroaster, has been characterized by atrocious barbarities. The constant oppression and tyranny which they have endured from the Mussulmans, have, of course, greatly thinned their numbers. Two centuries had not elapsed from the invasion, before the greater part of the population was converted to Islamism. In the tenth century of the Christian era, remnants of the Zoroastrian population were to be found only in the provinces of Fars and Kerman, and the reader may form some idea of the rate at which that remnant declined, when it is stated that while it numbered about a hundred years ago, one hundred thousand souls, it does not at present exceed seven thousand.

To Yezd and the twenty-four surrounding villages, these Zoroastrians of Persia are now almost exclusively confined. From accounts furnished to the writer by trustworthy authority, there were in the year 1854, in the above-mentioned city and its surrounding villages, one thousand houses or families, comprising a population of 6658 souls of whom 3310 were males and 3348 females. Of these about twenty or twenty-five were merchants, but by far the larger number gained a poor subsistence as tillers of the soil. A few of the poorest class worked as artizans, brick-layers, carpenters, weavers, or followed other mechanical occupations. At Kirman the number of Parsees does not exceed four hundred and fifty, while in the capital of Persia (Teheran), there are only about fifty merchants of this race. A small number of the poorer class, are however employed as gardeners in the palace of the Shah, and at Shiraz a few families are found in the grade of shopkeepers.

Within the past one hundred and fifty years four several revolutions have greatly conduced to the destruction of the Zoroastrian population of Kirman, which is now reduced to the very insignificant number before mentioned. The Gilji Afghans, who had long groaned under the misrule of Persia, determined at last to emancipate themselves, and raised the standard of rebellion under an able chief of the tribe named Meer Vais, who speedily subdued Candahar. The Persian monarch, Sultan Hussein, unable to reduce them by force of arms sent emissaries to persuade them into submission; but his mission was treated with contempt and the Afghan chief determined to invade Persia at the earliest opportunity. This soon presented itself, and at the moment when the north-eastern frontier of the kingdom was threatened by the Abdalli Afghans of Herat, and the Arabian ruler of Muscat was seizing the lands in the Gulf, Mahamood, who had succeeded his father Meer Vais in the government of Candahar, carried out his sire's resolve, and boldly invaded the empire which had so long oppressed his nation.

The following account by Sir John Malcolm of the Afghan leader's first entry into Persia, gives a terrible picture of the misery to which the inhabitants of Kirman were subjected on this occasion alike from the invaders and their rulers. "He (Mahamood) resolved to penetrate that country by the province of Kirman, preferring a march over the desert of Seistan to the obstacles which presented themselves in every other direction. Though he took every precaution to surmount the difficulties of the march, he lost many men and horses; but his appearance was so unexpected, and his force so considerable, that the city and province of Kirman immediately submitted to his arms. This ready acknowledgment of his authority did not save the inhabitants from suffering the most intolerable oppression, and it was with joy they learnt that Lootf Aly Khan had left the sea coast and was hastening to their relief. That chief, who had collected a considerable force, attacked and defeated the Afghan Prince, and compelled him to fly to Candahar. Kirman, however, was only exposed, by this victory, to a repetition of what it had before suffered; and when Lootf Aly Khan marched from that province, it was difficult to say whether the invasion of the Afghans or the advance of the Persian army to their relief had been most ruinous to its inhabitants." During this invasion by the Gilji Afghans, the Zoroastrians of Kirman drank to the full their share in the cup of suffering, and it was possible, that they were made the special objects of the vengeance taken by the troops of Lootf Aly Khan. At all events, on this occasion their numbers were greatly thinned either by massacre or conversion.

In the second invasion of Persia by Mahamood, he raised levies from among the Zoroastrians of both the provinces of Kirman and Yezd, persuading them to join his banner by appealing to their miseries. They were reminded of their ancestors and their wrongs, and urged to seize the opportunity, which was placed within their reach, of obtaining at once honour and revenge. The proposal seems to have been readily accepted, in the hope that the success of the Afghan Chief might alleviate the oppression to which they were constantly subjected under Persian rule. It is unnecessary to follow Mahamood in his various successes in this campaign, or to describe his final victory at, and capture of Ispahan. How the Zoroastrians who formed a portion of the army of Mahamood, fared at the hands of the chief in the hour of victory, we are altogether ignorant. We are not even told what became of them afterwards, but can rightly guess, that however valuable may have been their services, they received little substantial reward from a Mahomedan chief, and when we look at the condition of their descendants, we are tempted to conjecture, that they probably received the reverse of what they had deserved.

It is stated again, that in the reign of Nadir Shah, and that of his successor, the remnants of this persecuted race were again presented with the alternative of death or conversion. Moreover, about seventy-five years ago, when Agra Mahomed Khan Kujur, conquered Kirman in a war with Lootf Aly Khan Zund, many of the Zoroastrian race were put to the sword by that mereiless barbarian. When these various eireumstanees are taken into eonsideration, it ceases to be a matter for wonder that a population numbering very reeently many thousands of people, should have been redueed nearly to extinetion, by the cruelties of sueeessive tyrants. The eity of Kirman, even at this day, proves, by the numberless ruins of its fire-temples, that it must have been, at no very remote period, the abode of a eonsiderable population of the Zoroastrian persuasion.

To expeet that after the revolutions, persecutions, and oppressions, to whieh the small remnant of the deseendants of the aneient Persians have been subjeeted, they should to-day possess any of their religious books or be well-informed respeeting the tenets of their religion, would be unreasonable. Among all the vieissitudes of their raee, they have adhered in the most praiseworthy manner to the form of faith whieh deseended to them from their aneestors, and they pretend to nothing more. At one time the Parsees in India believed, that their eo-religionists in Persia eould furnish them with eopies of their ancient books, whieh were not possessed by those in Hindoostan and that they might be able to enlighten them on matters of their faith. But this delusion was not of long duration. The accounts of their condition, given by European travellers, as well as by the Iranees, who have visited India in our times, set all expectation at rest on the above point, and prove that instead of imparting wisdom, the Zoroastrians of the father-land now need advice and instruction from those in India.

They have it is true their fire-temples (thirty-four of them, including great and small, are situated in Yezd and its vicinity), but they have no ancient liturgical books among them, beyond those in the possession of their brethren in Hindoostan. Professor Westergard of Copenhagen, who visited Persia in the year 1843, writes to his friend Dr. Wilson of Bombay as follows, on this subject :—" I stopped at Yezd eleven days, and though I often went out among them, I did not see more than sixteen or seventeen books in all ; two or three copies of the Vendidad Sadé, and the Izeshiné (which they call Yaçn), and six or seven of the Khordé Avasta, of which I got two, and part of a third. These, besides part of the Bundesh, and part of another Pehelvi Book, were all I could get, though I tried hard to obtain more, especially part of the Izeshne with a Pehelvi, or as they say, Pazund translation, of which there is only one copy in Europe, at Copenhagen." The same learned traveller speaking of the Zoroastrians now residing in Kirman says; "The Gabres here are more brutalized than their brethren at Yezd. They had only two copies of the Vendidad and Yaçna, but a great many of the Khordé Avasta, which however they would not part with. No one here can read Pehelvi. They complain that when Aga Mahomed Khan gave the town up to indiscriminate plunder and slaughter, most of their books were destroyed, and great numbers of the race were killed."

We have thus seen how wretched is the general condition of the Zoroastrians now in Persia. The few who can be called rich belong to the merchant class, and besides these, there are perhaps none who can be said to be in good circumstances, while the great majority are in a state of extreme poverty. The Parsees of Bombay, who are much pained at the ignorance and wretched condition of this people, have of late been engaged in devising means for their relief. Schools have recently been established, where instruction is gratuitously imparted to their children; the Parsees of Bombay having wisely considered that the spread of education among their brethren in Persia will prove the surest harbinger of future good.

One of the severest oppressions under which these people suffer is the levy of the poll-tax, called *jujia*, to which they are subjected. The Moslem population is free from this tax: all "unbelievers" residing in the kingdom are, however, compelled to pay it. The Armenians, the Jews, and the Parsees, therefore, have to submit to the obnoxious impost. The Armenians residing at Tabriz, and in those parts of Persia contiguous to the Russian frontier, are exempt from the payment of this tax through the influence of the Russian Government; but those residing in other provinces have nothing left but to submit to the exaction.

The distress to which these races are driven to meet this tax is deplorable. We have no means of knowing the amount of impost which the Armenians and Jews are required to pay; but it has been ascertained that according to imperial order, the annual tax levied on the Parsees is 667 tomans.* As is the case,

* A toman is equal to ten shillings sterling.

however, in all Oriental kingdoms, the under-governors or collectors and magistrates, enhance the amount by their own commissions on it, and consequently the sum required to be paid by these poor people very often amounts to 2,000 tomans. According to statistics supplied to the writer from authentic sources, it appears that about a thousand grown up Parsees are required to pay the tax; of these, two hundred are able to bear the burden without difficulty; four hundred pay it with great inconvenience, while the rest are unable to pay it at all, even at the point of the sword.

Upon the annual collection of the tax, the scene presented before the homes of those who are unable to pay it, is most terrible to witness. Unheard of cruelties are practised in the hopeless attempt to extort the money. Some, as a last resource to save themselves from torture, give up their religion and embrace the faith of Mahomed, in which case they are exempted from payment of the tax. Others, who dare not violate their consciences, abandon their homes to escape the clutches of the tax-gatherer, leaving their wives and children in misery and want. Ground down to poverty, it is not strange that they should be unable to pay anything in the shape of taxes. In this miserable condition the Zoroastrians of Persia look towards their co-religionists in India for rescue from such oppression. A few who have found their way to Bombay, often put the question, "Can nothing be done to relieve our countrymen in Persia by the interference of the British ambassador at the court of Teheran at the instance of the influential Parsees of Bombay? The court of St. Petersburgh and other European powers have obtained various rights and privileges for the Christian inhabitants of Persia, and why cannot the English do so for the Parsees?"

It is not to be concealed that the Persian Government has very negligently observed its promise in regard to the Christians inhabiting its dominions. In the capital, where these people are immediately under the protection of the ambassadors of the Christian courts, their condition is comparatively comfortable, but in the provinces they are a prey, equally with the Jews and the Parsees, to the tyranny of the local governors, and the fanatic race among whom they dwell. Could the Zoroastrians, however, be in some way represented at the Persian court, their circumstances would probably be ameliorated. As it is, their wrongs have seldom been heard at the head-quarters of the government. The will of a Persian monarch is his law, and if the present sovereign, Nussroodin Shah, were to issue a simple edict against this obnoxious tax, which is to the poor Zoroastrian the cause of his greatest misery, he would be conferring a great and lasting boon upon the descendants of the most ancient inhabitants of his country.

The treatment which the Zoroastrians endure at the hands of other subjects of the Persian monarchy, is harsh and oppressive. They are contemptuously styled "Gabres," and experience from the Persians much the same sort of treatment as the low caste Mahar in India receives at the hands of the high caste Hindoo. A Mahomedan, who, without prejudice to himself, holds intercourse with every other caste, considers the touch of a "Gabre" as an impurity, and the latter is consequently debarred from following such occupations as are likely to bring him into contact with his oppressor.

Many other causes stand in the way of a Zoroastrian gaining an easy livelihood. In trade, credit must often be given to the purchaser, and the extreme difficulty which Zoroastrians find in recovering their claims from "true believers," is a great bar to a hearty or effective pursuit of commerce. "The Mahomedan law against debtors," says Sir John Malcolm, "is sufficiently severe, but the law is in no point favourable to what are termed in its language, unbelievers." We see it mentioned on the same authority, that an eminent Christian merchant, who resided many years in Persia, and who enlightened Europe by his observations on that country, states that nothing but the establishment of the Urf or customary law, which is administered by the secular magistrates, could enable a person not of the Mahomedan faith to carry on any commercial transactions in Persia. The bigotry of the priests, and the only law which they administer, that of the Koran and its traditions, would operate to deprive him of every hope of justice. When an application was made to the Court of Sherrah (by a non-believer) against a Mahomedan bankrupt, he was so sheltered under its forms and prescriptive laws, that it was declared impossible to attach his goods for the payment of his debts.

Of other instances of the shameless injustice of the laws, against those who do not adopt the national religion of Persia, one deserves prominent notice. If a rich man dies, any distant relative who may have embraced Mahomedanism, ean elaim his property in preference to the deceased's own lawful children. Sueh is the justice administered in Persia, and so shameless is it, that eomment upon it is rendered unneeessary.

Not only are the civil rights of a Parsee unprotected, but in every respect his position is one of eonstant peril. If a Mahomedan, whether from bigotry or malice, kills a Parsee or Jew, or any "unbeliever," there is no redress. The culprit is either slightly fined, as the price of a "kaffir's" life is very lightly estimated, or acquitted on some trivial pretext. The mention of a few late instances of the kind will suffice. An Armenian resident of Tabriz was killed by a Moslem. The murderer was fined seven Tomans (three pounds ten shillings) and the sum offered to the heirs of the deeeased. The latter declined to accept it, and demanded that a punishment should be inflicted on the offender equal to the guilt of his crime, but these remonstrances were unheeded, and the murderer was set at large to glory in having shed the blood of a kaffir. At Yezd two Parseés were murdered by some Mahomedans. The criminals were paupers and unable to pay a fine. They were consequently set at liberty, the judge declaring it unjust to imprison the followers of the true faith for merely laying violent hands on simple kaffirs. How justice is reversed in the case of the murder of a Mahomedan will be presently seen. A Jew had a pecuniary demand upon a Mahomedan, and the latter refusing to pay it, both of them had recourse to blows, in which the Mogul lost his life. In this case, as the victim was a Mahomedan, the fine was one thousand tomans, with imprisonment for some months. In short, a Parsee may be murdered or maltreated, and insulted to any extent, by a Mahomedan with open impunity. The Mahomedan law is founded on the Koran, and the administrators of it are the Mullas or priests, and the decision is, on principle, ever given against the "unbeliever," who is either in the position of a complainant or defendant.

The sanctuary of the fire-temples and towers of silence of the Parsees is often invaded, and any appeal to the authorities by the injured race is almost invariably treated with contempt or altogether unheeded. Rare instances do, however, occur when justice is done to the aggrieved, but when this exception is made, the success gained only serves as a pretext for further mischief. An instance of the kind occurred a few years since. A Parsee of Kirman having suffered an injury at the hands of a Mahomedan priest, appealed to the Shah of Teheran, and the Mulla was immediately summoned before the court and ordered to give immediate satisfaction for the wrong he had done. The Mahomedan, though forced at the time to comply with the mandate of authority, eagerly watched for an opportunity when he could revenge himself upon his enemy with impunity. In Persia all laws remain in abeyance on the death of a monarch till a successor is raised to the throne. During this interregnum, people do not consider themselves answerable for their crimes, and no notice can legally be taken of their conduct. The Mulla, therefore, thought that period an excellent opportunity for allaying his thirst for revenge, and on the death of the Shah, he endeavoured to stir up the Mahomedan mob to kill every unbeliever in Kirman as a work enjoined upon them by their holy Koran. The Parsees became, of course, the first victims of the infuriated mob, and many of them were killed.

Such instances are not of rare occurrence.

It is said that the present Shah and his ministers are not guilty of injustice, but, as must be the case in all despotic states, there is under their government no uniform system of law for the guidance and regulation of the conduct of officers entrusted with the administration of justice and security of the lives and property of the subject. The principal check upon such officers, says a well-known author, is the dread of superiors to whom the injured may always appeal. It is easier, however, to explain the duties than to describe the conduct of men, who regulate their actions by the varying dispositions of the despot of the day, and are active and just, or corrupt and cruel, as he happens to be vigilant and virtuous, or avaricious and tyrannical. That the majority of the sovereigns who have sat on the throne of Persia have been of the latter class is manifest, and we have no reason to suppose that future ones will prove more rich in virtue than their predecessors.

The physical and moral condition of the Parsees in Persia have remained unchanged since the time when they called the country their own. Centuries of oppression have not been able to destroy the strong, muscular and hardy appearance of the Zoroastrian. He is greatly superior in strength to the modern effeminate and luxurious Persian; and is ever willing to work could he find employment. Centuries of contact with a weak and idle race have not exercised any perceptible influence upon the habits of industry for which the ancestors of the Parsees were remarkable. The Zoroastrian is taught by his religion to earn his bread by the sweat of his brow, whereas the Molsem is taught to believe, that he will be the favoured of God by becoming a fakir and living on alms. It is a fact creditable to the blood which flows in Zoroastrian veins, that the race has not degenerated by contact with those by whom fate has surrounded them.

The same may be said of their moral conduct. The Mahomedans, their inveterate enemies, even admit this fact. Their women, the majority of whom belong to poor families, are remarkable for chastity; an unchaste woman is unheard of among them, while the men are noted for their moral conduct. In the garden adjoining the harem of the Shah, none are employed as gardeners but Zoroastrians, and this because of the national character for purity of these men. They are also remarkable for their love of truth, a virtue so highly extolled in their ancestors by historians both ancient and modern.

Never were the unhappy effects of misrule rendered more palpable than in the condition of the present remnant of our race remaining in the fatherland; while the state of the Parsees of Western India, as strikingly exemplifies the success and glory of an equitable and enlightened administration. But can we ourselves do nothing for our unfortunate co-religionists in Persia? Our community possesses considerable weight, and includes amongst its members, names known all over the world for their exertions in the cause of humanity, and the amelioration of the condition of their countrymen generally.

A deputation, therefore, of our race to the Persian Court, duly accredited by the English government, and presented by the British Ambassador at Teheran, might, we believe, remonstrate with success against the cruelties now practised upon our Zoroastrian brethren in Persia. The amount raised by the capitation tax now levied upon them, and which is attended by circumstances of so much cruelty, must be to the imperial revenue insignificant in the extreme, and it is not improbable that a dignified representation on the subject made by a suitable embassy from the Parsees of India might succeed in abolishing it. Persian Princes seldom know the true state of their subjects, and we cannot but think that our countrymen would reflect honour upon themselves by an adequate effort to relieve the miseries of our Zoroastrian brethren in the fatherland.

We are persuaded that the account we have attempted to give here of the remnant of the ancient Persian race, who have remained true to the religion of their fathers, and have continued on Persian soil, will not be without interest to the general reader. The instability of human grandeur receives no more striking illustration than is afforded by the overthrow of the great monarchies which ruled in Asia before the Christian era. Inheritors of the old glories of the Assyrian and Babylonian empires, the Persian power spread its dominion from the isles of Greece to the table-land of Thibet—from the Caspian Sea to the confines of India. The ruins of ancient Persepolis tell of the splendour and the power of the Magian princes. The remains of mighty causeways, cut step by step on the Bakhtyari mountains, which divide the valley of the Tigris from the plains of Ispahan, and form the natural defence on that side of the modern Moslem empire of Persia, tell of the passage of myriads of busy feet, and the march of heavy bodies of soldiery in ancient times, where now even the caravanserai dare not pass, and the wild robbers of the hills gain a precarious subsistence by plundering the plains, and by tending cattle, which form their only wealth. In short, here is a country, once the most powerful, groaning under fanatic and despotic rulers, while the few descendants of that proud ancient race are sunk into unnoticeable insignificance. All this, we again say, forcibly reminds us of the instability of human grandeur. To a Parsee, however, the decline and fall of the old Persian empire is a subject of peculiar interest. That strong feeling of association which binds to the present the memory of the past stages of a man's private existence—that same feeling presents vividly before our minds the memory of what our forefathers were. Our race in India enjoys all the blessings of an enlightened and liberal government—and our only wish is that our brethren in the Persian soil may also be as happy and fortunate as ourselves.

CHAPTER III.

MANNERS AND CUSTOMS.

Parsee population in India—How dispersed—Sects among the Parsees—Causes which led to the division—Domestic life of a Parsee family—Birth of a child—Consultation with the Astrologer as to the fortunes of the infant—Naming of children—Dress of a child—Its baptism into Zoroastrianism—Investiture of the Sudra and Kusti—Home and outdoor costume of a Parsee—Appearance and dress of females—Mode of living—Nature of food used by them—Mode of eating—Occasions for entertainments—Position of Parsee women—Marriage festivities—Mode of betrothal—Wedding and other ceremonies—Freedom of remarriage—Prohibition of bigamy—Rules regulating bigamy in certain cases—Funeral ceremonies—Mode of disposing of the dead bodies.

THE numerical strength of the followers of Zoroaster at the present day does not exceed 150,000 persons, including the Parsees of Persia. The greater number is found in Bombay, and in some of the cities of Gujerat, a province 200 miles to the north of that city. Parsees have also settled for the purposes of trade in Calcutta, and in other cities of British India, in China, and in other parts of Asia. The returns from the census of Bombay, taken on the night of the 20th of August, 1851, show that the number of Parsees in the island on that day was 110,544, of whom 68,754 were males, and 41,790 females, the proportion of the former to the latter being nearly seven to four. The following table classes the population according to age—

Under 2 years of age . . .	2,900
From 2 to 6 „ . . .	6,996
„ 7 to 13 „ . . .	9,509
„ 14 to 24 „ . . .	16,542
„ 25 to 34 „ . . .	20,366
„ 35 to 44 „ . . .	19,484
„ 45 to 54 „ . . .	18,000
„ 55 to 64 „ . . .	9,037
„ 65 to 74 „ . . .	5,967
„ 75 and above . . .	1,743
Total	110,544

When the above returns were made public the Parsees generally believed that they were inaccurate, and that the number given exceeded the real strength of the people. Let the fact be as it may, it can hardly be doubted that the Parsee population of to-day may fairly be estimated at the above figures; and, as the community is a healthful and thriving one, its increase is very rapid. On the general question of the propagation of the human race, "its power of increase," says John Stuart Mill, "is indefinite, and the actual multiplication would be extraordinarily rapid, if that power were exercised to the utmost. It never is exercised to the utmost; and yet in the most favourable circumstances known to exist, which are those of a fertile region colonized from an industrious and civilized community, population has continued, for several generations, independently of fresh immigration, to double itself in not much more than twenty years. That there is a capacity of multiplication in the human species beyond even this is evident if we consider how great is the ordinary number of children to a family where the climate is good, and early marriages usual; and how small a proportion of them die before the age of maturity, in the present state of hygienic knowledge, where the locality is healthy and the family inadequately provided with the means of living. It is a very low estimate of the capacity of increase if we only assume that, in a good sanitary condition of the people, each generation may be double the number of the generation which preceded it."

Now, though the Parsees have not paid so much attention to sanitary improvements as the English, they certainly approximate nearer to them on this point than any other race in India; and the mortality of children under the age of six years is twenty per cent. less among those of the Parsees than amongst those of other natives. The Parsees form twenty per cent. of the population of Bombay, while the rate of mortality is but 4·71 per cent.; and it cannot be doubted that under the protection of the British rule they have a tendency to multiply faster than any other of the races of India.

In Bombay, the increase has been very evident indeed. Fifteen or twenty years ago the Parsee population was confined to only a part of the fort and the native town. At the present time, the fort is almost wholly in their occupation, while numbers are spread in all directions through the island. They have no fear of being absorbed by the Hindoos or Mahomedans, intermarriages with others than those of their own community being not only distasteful to the people themselves, but prohibited by law.

The Parsees at Surat at one time greatly exceeded in number those of Bombay; but as the latter city became the great emporium of trade in Western India, the enterprising spirit of the people soon brought them down from Surat to that place, and the population at the old city, it is supposed, does not now exceed 20,000 souls.

At Broach and Nowsaree there are about 5,000 Zoroastrians, and the number at Ahmedabad, Dumaun, Gundavee, Oodwarra, Bulsar, and Billimora, as well as those who are scattered about for the purposes of trade, does not in all exceed 10,000. To these we must add about 6,000 Zoroastrians in Persia, and we have the whole Parsee population, which, as we have said above, does not exceed 150,000.

The Parsees of India are divided into two sects, the Shensoys and the Kudmis. They do not differ on any point of faith as the Protestants do from the Romanists, nor does the distinction between them at all resemble that which divides the different castes of the Hindoos, or the Shyas and Soonees among the Mahomedans. Their form of worship and religious ceremonies are the same in every respect. They freely mingle in society, and in every relation of life, and the dispute is solely confined to a quarrel as to the correct chronological date for the computation of the era of Zezdezird, the last King of the ancient Persian monarchy. The difference has, as yet, been productive of no further inconvenience than arises from the variation of a month in the celebration of the festivals.

The Shenshoy sect greatly outnumbers the Kudmis. Out of a population of 110,000 souls, there are hardly 10,000 Kudmis. But the smallness of their number has been no bar to their gaining a position in the community, or to their advancement in life. Within the last twenty-five years, a number of the most influential Parsees belonged to this sect, and even at the present day it numbers some of the most distinguished merchants. The late Framjee Cowasjee, than whom a more enlightened Parsee never lived, was of this sect. In our day this class is represented by the highly respected Framjee Nusserwanjee, Esq., the members of the Cama family, enlightened, liberal, enterprising, and wealthy merchants, and the Dadysett family, whose ancestors were highly renowned for their public spirit and generosity.

The more numerous, class, the Shenshoys, is represented by Sir Jamsetjee Jejeebhoy, Bart., and many rich families. How this division arose remains to be explained. There was no such distinction whatever among the Zoroastrians when in the peaceful possession of their fatherland. It has resulted from the exile of their descendants in India. In the year of Yezdezird 1090, or nearly 200 years ago, one Jamasp, a learned Zoroastrian from Persia, arrived at Surat to undertake the instructions of the Mobeds, or priests; and he is said to have been the first to discover that his co-religionists in India differed with their brethren of Iran in the calculation of time by full one month, but no great importance was attached to the point, and all went smoothly as before. But in the year of Yezdezird 1114, or 1746 of Christ, an Iranee, named Jemshid, attaching to himself a few *mobeds* or priests, and by adopting the notion imported by Jamasp, formed the Kudmi Sect; the bulk of the people however adhered to their former views.

For a time the difference was neither productive of argument nor collision among the people, but about thirty years ago Bombay became the theatre of a great discussion on this point. The Kudmis, headed by their high priest Mulla Firoz, fought for the new era, while, on the other side, the mass of the people, headed by a then very popular and influential member of the community, the late Shet Cursetjee Manackjee,* was arrayed against them. Public meetings were held, to which learned Moguls and others were invited, and where many highly animated discussions took place. Newspapers were started as the organs of the respective parties, and a good deal of violent writing was indulged in, but no satisfactory result ensued from the controversy.

This celebrated discussion is known to every Parsee by the designation of the "Kubeesa Controversy." The men of the present day attach, however, little importance to the subject, and prefer quietly pursuing their ordinary avocations to re-opening a question which could lead to no satisfactory results. The chief importance of the matter arises from the fact that a Parsee when he prays has to repeat the year, month, and day on which he offers his petition,† therefore the mention

* The father of Mr. Manockjee Cursetjee, who visited England some years ago, and who is now third Judge of the Court of Small Causes at Bombay.

† The names of the Parsee days and months are as follows:—

Days:—1, Hormazd; 2, Bahman; 3, Ardebehest; 4, Shurever; 5, Aspundad; 6, Khordad; 7, Amerdad; 8, Depadur; 9, Adur; 10, Ava; 11, Khorshed; 12, Mhor; 13, Teer; 14, of the date, is the only distinction between the prayer of a Kudmi and that of a Shenshoy, and the same difference exists in the keeping of the festivals which are common to both sects.*

Gosh; 15, Depmeter; 16, Meher; 17, Serosh; 18, Rashne; 19, Furvurdeen; 20, Behram; 21, Ram; 22, Guvad; 23, Depdin; 24, Din; 25, Ashasang; 26, Ashtad; 27, Asman; 28, Zamiad; 29, Maharespiand; 30, Aniran.

Months:—1, Furvurdeen; 2, Ardibehest; 3, Khurdad; 4, Tir; 5, Amerdad; 6, Sherevur; 7, Meher; 8, Aban; 9, Adur; 10, Deh; 11, Behman; 12, Aspendadmad.

* As a work of this nature would be incomplete without some account of the Parsee festivals, the following description of them, abridged from the *Bombay Times Calendar*, is given for the information of the reader:—

Pappati, or New Year's Day.—Among the festivals observed by the Parsees, the first and universally kept is the Pappati, or new year's day. This day is celebrated in honour of Yezdezerd, the last king of the Sassanide dynasty, who was dethroned by Khalif Omar about A.D. 640. The ancient Persians reckoned a new era from the accession of each successive monarch, and as Yezdezerd had no successor, the date of his accession to the throne has been brought down to the present time, thus making their current year 1227. In their calculations of the year only 365 days are allowed; the leap year is unknown to them, though there are records which prove that in every 120 years one month was added to the period, to correspond with the solar year. The year is divided into twelve months of thirty days each, and five days, or "gathas," as they are called, are added at the end to make up the deficiency. On this day the Parsees rise early, and dress themselves in new suits of clothes, and those piously disposed say their prayers in their private residences, or attend the fire-temples, where a large congregation is gathered. After prayers the Parsees visit their friends and relations, when the "Hamma-i-jour," or "joining

Having furnished in a foot note an account of the Parsee religious festivals, we pass on to

of hands," is performed. This ceremony is a sort of greeting, corresponding to the European fashion of wishing each other a happy new year. Their friends and relations are invited to breakfast. The morning being thus occupied, they spend the rest of the day in their country houses and clubs, where feasting, rejoicing, and nautch-parties are kept up till a late hour. Alms are also given to the poor in the course of the day, and new suits of clothes are presented to their servants and dependants.

Khordad-Sal.—The second of the Parsee festivals is the "Khordad-Sal" day, or the anniversary of the birth of their prophet Zoroaster, who was born in the city of Rai in the north of Persia, in the reign of Darius Hystaspis, about 520 years before Christ, according to Greek writers.

Amardad-Sal.—This holiday, which falls on the day immediately after the preceding festival, appears to have no origin in the books of the Parsees. It is merely kept up as a continuation of the "Khordad-Sal;" no religious ceremonies are required, and the day is always spent in the enjoyment of pleasures.

Furrohurdin Jasan.—This day is set apart for the performance of ceremonies for the dead, Furrohur meaning soul or spirit. This holiday is kept with some slight variations in other parts of India. The Parsees are enjoined by their religion to preserve the memory of their dead by annual religious ceremonics performed in the house; but such of their friends who die on long voyages or in unknown places, and the date of whose death cannot be positively ascertained are, according to the forms of their religion, honoured by sacred rites on this day.

Ardibehest Jasan.—This festival, as its name implies, is maintained in honour of Ardibehest Amsaspund, the controlling angel over the sacred fire, that element being one of the symbols of worship. The fire temples are crowded this day, and prayers offered to the Supreme Deity.

the description of the domestic life of the people. Beginning with the infant, we may

The Nowroz.—The fifth on our list is the celebrated Nowroz, called by some the Nowroz-i-Jamshid, or the Nowroz-i-Sultan, the King's day. This celebrated festival falls generally on the 21st day of March, and is coeval with our vernal equinox, and the Mukhr Saccaranti of the Hindus. This day is observed by the modern Persians, the Arabs, the Turks, and several other Asiatic nations, for the computation of the solar year, and for state purposes, such as the collection of revenue, and the arrangements for the agricultural operations of the year. Eastern writers date the origin of this festival from the time of Jamshid, the third king of the Peshdadian dynasty of Persia, and our own Western writers are not disposed to doubt this statement. Jamshid is supposed to have flourished, according to Bailey, 3,209 years before Christ; the Shah Nameh celebrates him as the first prince of his race who introduced civilization among mankind, and established the computation of time. If we are to believe the host of Persian writers, the exquisite bas-reliefs at the ruins of Persepolis—still visible in all their pristine beauty after a lapse of two thousand years—are representations of the court of Jamshid, more especially on the festival of Nowroz. The sculptures at this remarkable place, indeed, contain representations of the courts of ancient Persia, with their long train of attendants bringing in offerings to the feet of the monarchs; and as the Nowroz is a sort of "revenue settlement" day, when the chiefs of the different provinces lay their annual contributions before the throne, and are allowed audience with the monarch, the idea of a part of the Persepolitan bas-reliefs being a picture of some ancient king of Persia holding his court on the day of the Nowroz, does not appear to be without a good foundation. In Persia this festival is kept up for several days with unusual pomp by all the inhabitants, whether Mahomedans or Parsees. In India it is simply a day of rejoicing.

Ava Ardui Sur Jasan.—Ava, in the Zend text, is the name

mention that it is introduced into the world on the ground-floor of the house, to which the

of the angel who presides over the sea, and this "Jasan" or festival is held in his honour. The Parsees are simply required on this day to approach the sea-shore, or any stream of water, and chant the prayers which are written in Zend; but, owing to their long residence in this country, they have borrowed many Hindoo rites in the observance of this holiday, and offerings of sugar, cocoa-nut, flowers, &c., to the sea, on this day, are not uncommon. The better informed portion of the community, however, do not join with their brethren in these superstitious acts. In Bombay a fair is held on the Esplanade in honour of this festival.

Addar Jasan.—Addar, another synonyme for fire, is the name by which the ninth month of the Parsee year is called. This is the most religious of the twelve months, and the ninth day of that month is held in great respect and sanctity. On this day the fire-temples are very much crowded, and offerings of sandal-wood are made to the sacred flame, and money distributed among the priests.

Besides the above, the festivals of the Parsees are the Meher Jasan, the Boman Jasan, and a few others of less importance, all of which are partially observed.

The *Mooktads* is the name of a ceremony which is performed at the end of the Parsee year. It consists of a pile of brass or silver vessels filled with water and raised above the ground on iron stools. Flowers and fruits are placed there, and religious ceremonies in honour of the dead are performed before the Mooktads. A society for religious reform, which has been lately established among the Parsees, has denounced this ceremony in no respectful terms. According to the tracts published by these reformers, the Parsee Scriptures only require that the last ten days of the year should be spent in deeds of charity, prayers, and freedom from worldly pursuits; they add further, that the ceremony of the brass and silver vessels, &c., is borrowed entirely from the Hindoos.

mother is conveyed as soon as she is seized with the pains of labour, and she remains there for forty days, at the expiration of which period, after undergoing purification, she is allowed to appear in the family as before.

For five days after the birth of the child the mother is fed simply with conjee or other light food, and the infant is sustained chiefly by sugar and water, given to it by means of a wick. The exact period of birth is carefully noted down, and five days after the event, or as soon as convenient, an astrologer is invited, who is either a Brahmin or a Parsee priest, to cast the nativity of the child. He begins by drawing on a wooden board a set of hieroglyphics in chalk, and his dexterity in counting and recounting the stars under whose region or influence the child is declared to be born, is marvelled at by the superstitious creatures thronging around him. All the relatives of the child press forward to hear the astrologer predict the future life and prospects of the babe. The fellow, who thoroughly understands the worth of his forecastings, gives out, with an air of satisfaction, that the child is destined to hold a distinguished position in the community! He has first, however, to enumerate the names which the child may bear, and the parents have the right to make choice of one of them.

The astrologer is then consulted as to the influence the child will exert upon the fortunes of the father, the mother, brother, and family generally. The pretender gravely delivers himself in some such strain as this, "The child really is a fortunate one. To its father it has brought increased respectability and wealth; the mother will be very fortunate. By the birth of this babe there will be increased affection between the husband and wife. With its brothers and sisters it will be on good terms when of age." The men generally laugh at the absurdity of this stuff, but the condition of the Parsee females is not yet sufficiently advanced to make them conscious of its folly. The spread of education, now happily commenced, will soon purge away such superstitious trash from among them.

The costume of the Parsees is well adapted for the hot climate of the country. The dress of a child, till it is seven years of age (when it has to be invested with the sudra and kusti, or the sacred shirt and cord) is exceedingly simple and becoming. It consists of a single piece or garment called the "jubhla," which extends from the neck to the ankles. It is a sort of loose shirt, through which the head and arms are passed. The topee, or skull-cap, covers the head, and completes the dress. The holiday attire is exceedingly elegant and fanciful. The *jubhla* and *topee* are bravely embroidered with China silks, or with gold and silver lace. Pearls, emeralds, and other jewels are also arranged about the person.

A writer in one of the magazines lately published at Delhi thus describes a band of Parsee children at holiday time. "Both sexes take a more than ordinary pride and pleasure in the children, who appear abroad on high days and holidays in all the bravery of rich silks, jewels, embroidery, and variegated colours; and with their handsome attire, and smiling intelligent faces, as they sport about, or are driven along in the parental carriage, prettier or more interesting little creatures can nowhere be found." Another writer says, "Though Parsees take particular pride in extravagantly adorning their children, the most fastidious European eye would not take offence at their costume, unless it be an apprehension of dread for the cupidity which would desire the costly ornaments that are shown to such advantage."

The investiture of the child with the *sudra* and *kusti*, or its baptism, if we may be allowed the expression, into the Zoroastrian religion, takes place, according to religious injunctions, after it has attained the age of six years and three months. The "jubhla" is then thrown off, and the *sudra* and *kusti* are put on, which is not done without an appropriate ceremony. After washing and undergoing certain ceremonies, the child is seated before the *dastoor*, or high priest, and those who are invited to witness the ceremony. The dastoor then pronounces a benediction, and with due forms the emblems of Zoroastrianism are put on.

The *sudra* is made of linen or linen gauze, or net, while the *kusti* is a thin woollen cord, or cincture of seventy-two threads.* The former is called, in the language of the Avasta, *Suttehur Pesunghem*, which means "The garment of the good and beneficial way." The *kusti* is passed round the waist three times, and tied with four knots, during the chanting of a sort of hymn. At the first knot the person says "There is only one God, and no other is to be compared with him;" at the

* These threads represent the seventy-two Has or chapters of the Sacred Book of the Parsees, called Izashné.

second, "The religion given by Zurtosht is true;" at the third, "Zurtosht is the true Prophet, and he derived his mission from God;" at the fourth and last, "Perform good actions, and abstain from evil ones."

The house costume of a Parsee consists of a long muslin shirt (*sudra*) and girdle, with a waistcoat of white cloth or chintz, loose trousers of cotton, slippers, and a skull-cap of China silks. When going abroad he puts on an *angrakha*, or loose ungirdled tunic, which is thrown over the muslin shirt, and the sleeves of which are twice the length of the arm, and are folded up in wrinkles above the wrist. The turban, which is generally of a dark chocolate colour, of a fanciful pattern, forms the out-door covering for the head, and is worn over the skull-cap.

The rich wear silk trousers, stockings, and English shoes. The full-dress of a Parsee consists, in addition to the above, of a *jama* of white linen and a *pichoree*. The sleeves and upper portion of the former are of the same fashion as the *angrakha*, but the skirt is full, and resembles that of an English lady's gown. The *pichoree* is a long cloth about a yard wide, and many yards in length, and is passed round the waist in successive folds. This dress is only used at funeral and wedding parties; but the Parsees have thought it becoming to assume it when invited to an English ball, or to Government-house.

The dress of the Kudmi sect of the Parsees does not differ from that of the Rushmis. A few priests of the former wear a peculiar dress of their own, in imitation of that used by their late high priest, Mulla Firoz, which, in a great measure, resembles the dress of an Armenian or a Turk. The Parsee priests generally adopt the same dress as laymen, with the exception of the turban, which is of folded white cloth.

The Parsee women are generally graceful and well formed; fair in complexion, and of a pleasing countenance. They are robbed of a part of their beauty by the custom of concealing their hair under a thin cloth of white linen, called *mathabana*, or the head-binder. The hair is gathered into a knot at the back of the head, and tied with the ends of the *mathabana*. Like the men, they put on the shirt and the *kusti*, and wear silk trousers. Their *sarees*, or outer dress, are several yards in length, and are generally of bright coloured silks or satins, sometimes embroidered with fanciful design, or fringed with deep gold lace, for great occasions. This dress is first folded round the waist, covering the lower limbs, and the remainder is gracefully thrown over the head, from which it falls upon the right arm. Under the *saree* they wear a silk vest, with short sleeves, called the *kanchri* or *choli*. A Parsee woman, whether rich or poor, has ornaments to adorn her person. The rich possess jewels in the shape of the necklace, the nose-ring, composed of three large pearls, with an emerald pendant, and bangles of pearls, gold and brilliants for the wrist and ankle. They sometimes may be seen in slippers worked in pearls.

The dress of the modern Parsees of India differs from that worn by their ancestors in Persia, and by their present co-religionists in that country. They have adopted the present costume in accordance with their agreement with the Hindoo princes who received them in India, and to this is attributable the great resemblance of the *angrakha* and turban of the men, and the *saree* of the women, to the dress of the Hindoos of Guzerat.

The Parsee mode of life may be described as half-European and half-Hindoo. Every year advancing in civilization and enlightenment, they copy more closely English manners and modes of living. The Greek historians remarked, that of all nations, the ancient Persians were generally distinguished by their readiness in imitating foreign manners and customs, this peculiarity their descendants retain to the present day. During their sojourn in Guzerat, they adopted the language, dress, and other social customs of that country, and they are now being drawn into European manners and customs. The educated and influential classes have already adopted in their domestic life the comforts, conveniences, and elegancies, and we may add, the costliness, of the European style.

The domestic arrangements of their residences have also of late undergone a vast change. Their houses are generally built in good taste, upon well-conceived plans, and are admirably ventilated; their villas or garden-houses are the best in Bombay. The reception-rooms are richly furnished and decorated, and the walls adorned with landscape and historical pictures, while the glory of a Parsee house is to be one blaze of light from lamps and chandeliers.

A great improvement is now observable among the Parsees in their manner of eating. Formerly they sat on the ground at meals like the Hindoos, and took their food out of one brazen dish, on which the viands were spread in confusion. Now the table and chair, with all the accompaniments of a European dinner, are put in requisition. When large parties are given, the table is spread exactly in the English mode, instead of as formerly, when hundreds would be grouped upon the floor, each eating his dinner from a plantain leaf!

The Parsees, properly speaking, eat three times a day. In the morning, soon after their ablutions, they sit down to breakfast,* which consists of tea, bread and butter, and eggs. Between twelve and one dinner or tiffin is served, at which rice and curry, with mutton, vegetables, and fish, are the principal dishes. The poorer classes are, however, content with simple rice and curry. Between four and five in the afternoon tea is again prepared, and the time for supper is between eight and ten. This is the most substantial meal of the day, and wines are then consumed in large quantities by those who can afford them; but it is a fact creditable to the sobriety of the Parsees

* The Parsee is enjoined before each meal to acknowledge with grateful thanks, the kindness of Providence in providing him with his daily bread.

generally, that they drink no intoxicating liquors during the day.

The males take their meals apart from the females. The male members of the family either sup together or separately, and the female members do the same. This custom is certainly derived from the Hindoos, as the ancient Persians observed no such distinction. History fully proves that the ancestors of the Parsees not only dined with their mothers, wives, and sisters, but took their ladies out with them to feasts. At a dinner, said to have been given by Amintus, king of Macedon, to the Persian ambassador, at his court, the latter, in acknowledgment of some toast, is said to have expressed his grief that no ladies were present, as was the custom in his own country, for without their fair companions the happiness of the company could not be said to be complete. Many educated Parsees, however, have commenced the practice of taking their meals with their fair partners, an introductory step certainly in the right direction.

The Parsee women occupy a much more honourable position than either their Hindoo or Mahomedan sisters. The Parsees in general are good and affectionate husbands, and discharge faithfully their duties towards their wives, while the latter are not unconscious of theirs towards their lords, and hence most families lead a peaceable and very happy life. In a great number of cases the husbands are much influenced by their wives, and considering the present state of education among the latter, it is remarkable that such exceptions ever should exist. Though the Parsee ladies are not seen in society, it is not to be supposed that their life at home is spent in entire seclusion or in female company only, as is the case among the Hindoos and Mahomedans. At home they mix freely in the family,* join in the conversation and take part in other affairs without reserve, while during the day they are engaged in visiting and gossiping among themselves. They also find employment in making dresses for their children, in which they take much interest, also in working in embroidery and Berlin wool, an occupation introduced among them of late years only, but in which they have made considerable progress. The

* The members of a Parsee family often number by scores. The sons do not after their marriage live separately from their parents, and oftentimes in the same houses are to be seen the great grandfather and the great grandchildren. Sir Jamsetjee's family, including the aged and little ones, numbers about one hundred.

halls of the wealthy contain many exquisite specimens of this art, which constantly attract the admiration of European visitors. The females of the poorer classes are mostly engaged in the kitchen, attending to domestic matters, or in fetching water from the wells, which are generally situated at some distance from the house.

As a race the Parsees are highly social, and they embrace every opportunity of visiting or entertaining their friends and relations. A religious festival or holiday, a birthday or a marriage, are the great occasions for their social enjoyments. As an indication of the increasing intellectual taste of the Parsees, it may be noted that of late English music forms one of the amusements of their evening parties instead of the ugly and absurd *nautches* of native dancing girls, accompanied by musicians (save the mark!) who are no great masters of their profession, but who grin, nod, and stamp, and make horrible faces in their excitement, with a view to deceive the audience into the belief that they are absorbed in the spirit of their art!

The marriage festivities of the Parsees are very noteworthy. The marriages of children engage the earliest attention of the parents.

An Englishman's first care is the education of his children—a Parsee's their marriage. Some improvement has doubtless taken place in the matter of late, and a wiser practice may possibly soon supervene upon the old. The absurd custom of early marriage is to be traced to the sojourn of the Parsees in India.

According to the law of Zoroaster, a boy or girl ought not to be married before the age of fifteen, and this rule must have been observed by the ancient Persians; but among a number of customs which the Parsees in India adopted from the Hindoos, this one of early marriages may safely be included. Hindoos are most strictly enjoined by their *shasters* to have their girls married before they have attained the age of nine years, in failure whereof, great shame is attached to their parents. This idea of shame has been, to some extent, participated in by the Parsees, and hence the early marriage of their daughters. There are, besides this, other causes which have greatly contributed to the anxiety which exists among them as to the marriage of their children. As weddings are legitimate occasions for rejoicings and festivities, most of the wealthy are glad of the opportunities they afford for the display of their wealth in giving dinners and *nautch* parties on an extensive scale to their relatives, neighbours, friends, and acquaintances. On the other hand the women, who on these occasions invite their friends, have the gratification of displaying their jewellery and rich dresses, and so urge on the men in bringing about an early consummation of their wishes.

Under these circumstances, there is little chance that a Parsee gentleman should enter the family of his proposed partner in order to win her affections, or that he should obtain a wife of his own personal choice. To those unacquainted with Parsee manners and customs it will perhaps be startling to learn that instances are not wanting of the betrothal of a boy of three years of age to a girl of two. It may seem very ridiculous, but it is nevertheless a fact, that not later than fifteen or twenty years ago it was the custom in Bombay, and in some of the cities of Guzerat, to arrange or negociate for the marriage of children which had not even seen the light of this world; that is to say, if the respective wives of two friends became *enceinte*, they came to an understanding that if one bore a son and the other a daughter, the infants should be united in marriage.

This foolish system is, we believe, no longer

practised in Bombay; but instances of the kind still occur among the Parsees in some of the villages in Guzerat, where the march of enlightenment is not so rapid as it is in Bombay. A great change has taken place within the last fifteen or twenty years in Bombay, and though the majority of marriages are still celebrated while the children are very young, instances frequently occur of marriages of grown up boys and girls. The feeling of shame, which, in common with the Hindoos, was for a long time shared by the Parsees, has to a great degree disappeared, and it may, with some degree of confidence, be asserted that ten or twenty years hence, early marriages among the Parsees will be a thing of the past.

As this subject is likely to be interesting to the European reader, the writer feels that no apology is necessary for his entering minutely into the details of the marriage ceremony among the Parsees. Some of the priests, who have extensive acquaintance with influential families, follow the profession of match-makers. Having made due inquiries about the rank and position of the families possessing daughters to dispose of, they go amongst the families with sons who are candidates for the estate of matrimony, and endeavour to mate the two. The parents or guardians of the boy institute inquiries whether the parents of the girl pointed out to them are respectable persons.* On being satisfied that they are so, the match-maker's recommendation is favourably received, and direct negociation is opened with the parents of the girl by requesting them to furnish for a day or two the horoscope or birth-paper of the maiden, that the astrologer may be consulted as to the eligibility or otherwise of the match.

The horoscope of the boy, as well as that of the girl, is then handed over to the professor of astrology, in order that he may examine whether the "stars" of the proposed pair are favourable to the union, and whether it is likely to prosper. On the answer of this sage much depends. If he does not approve the match, but augurs that ill will arise from it, negociations are at once broken off; but if he shows no such apprehension, and prognosticates happiness for the pair, the proposal has advanced one important stage towards its accomplishment. The stars once declared

* In some cases the parents of the boy or girl commission some of the match-making priests to find out a proper match for their children.

favourable to the union, the parents of the boy and girl cause further inquiries to be made into each other's means, respectability, position, and connections in the community. The parents of the girl inquire particularly as to the amicability or otherwise of the mother of the future son-in-law, as, in a Parsee family, the happiness of the wedded girl depends greatly upon the behaviour of the mother-in-law towards her, the husband being, like herself, a minor.

When the heads of both families are satisfied as to the fitness of the match, the betrothal of the young people takes place, a propitious day for the celebration of which is named by the astrologer. There is no tedious ceremony attending the betrothal. The parents of the boy send a present of a dress for the girl, and those of the girl one for the boy. This exchange of presents makes the marriage contract "pucka" complete, and it cannot now be dissolved. There is no fixed period at which the marriage ceremony should necessarily be performed. It rests with the convenience of the parties, but the latest time at which the final ceremony is performed is a little before or immediately after the girl has arrived at the age of puberty. But instances are not wanting, as we have above stated, of both the betrothal and the marriage ceremony taking place while the bride and bridegroom are little more than infants.

The day for the celebration of the marriage is named of course by the astrologer. Certain days in the year are supposed to be propitious for the ceremony, and that is the reason why a foreigner during his stay in India is struck by the number of marriages taking place on the same day. During several days before the marriage, if the parties are rich, continual dinners and nautches are given to friends, both males and females, and many thousands of rupees are thus spent. It is also customary on such occasions for the parents and kinsmen of the bride and bridegroom to exchange presents of ornaments and rich dresses. To the bride ornaments of great value are presented by her father-in-law. The above practices, though little objectionable among those who can afford it, are extremely injurious to the poorer classes, who ruin themselves for the sake of imitating their richer neighbours. When their own means will not bear the expense which they are about to incur, the money lender is resorted to, and a loan secured on payment of so heavy a premium, that the man is frequently embarrassed during his whole life.

On the wedding-day large parties* are invited to their respective houses by the parents of the bride and bridegroom to witness the nuptial ceremony, which takes place in the evening after the custom of the Hindoos, and the promise given to the Raja of Sunjan by the ancestors of the present Parsees on their landing at that place. The gentlemen are accommodated with chairs and benches in the verandah and the two sides of the road facing the house where the ceremony is to be performed, while the apartments are gallantly left to the ladies. On this occasion the former dress in *Jamas* and *Pichoree*, the full costume of the Parsees, while the latter array themselves in dresses of the most rich and variegated colours, ornamented with gold and jewellery.

About sunset the whole of the bridegroom's party, both males and females, repair in procession to the house of the bride. The procession is headed by a European or native band of music, according to the means of the parties; the bridegroom, accompanied by the

* The wedding party in a highly respectable or wealthy family consists of from 500 to 1,000 persons, including males and females.

dustoors, then follow, after whom walk the male portion of the assembly, the female company bringing up the rear of the procession. When the whole of this party is accommodated at the bride's quarters, the nuptial ceremony is commenced soon after sunset. It generally takes place in a hall or spacious room on the ground-floor of the house, where a *galicha* or carpet is spread. The bride and bridegroom are seated close to each other on ornamented chairs, and facing them stand the *dustoors* or priests, who repeat the nuptial benediction first in the Zend and then in the Sanscrit,* of which the following is a short abstract,—"Know ye, that both of you have liked each other, and are therefore thus united. Look not with impious eye on other people, but always make it your study to love, honour, and cherish each other as long as both of you remain in this world. May quarrels never arise between you, and may your fondness for each other increase day by day. May you both learn to adhere to truth, and be always pure in your thoughts as well as actions, and always try to please the Almighty, who is the lover of Truth and

* The repetition of the benediction in Sanscrit, is in accordance with the promise given to the Hindoo Rajah, *vide* page 14.

Righteousness. Shun evil company, abstain from avarice, envy, and pride, for that is the road to destruction. Think not of other men's property, but try industriously, and without any dishonest means, to improve your own. Cultivate friendship between yourselves, and with your neighbours, and among those who are known to be good people. Hold out a helping hand to the needy and poor. Always respect your parents, as that is one of the first duties enjoined upon you. May success crown all your efforts. May you be blessed with children and grandchildren. May you always try to exalt the glory of the religion of Zoroaster, and may the blessings of the Almighty descend upon you."

The concluding ceremony of washing the toes of the bridegroom's feet with milk, and rubbing his face with his bride's cholee,* as well as other trivialities need not be mentioned here, as they are not enjoined by the Parsee religion, but are mere "grafts of Hindooism." When the above ceremonies are nearly concluded, bouquets of roses, or other beautiful and fragrant flowers, and little triangular packets of *pan soparee*,†

* Silk vest worn as a waist-coat.

† A kind of leaf and Betel-nut.

profusely gilded, are distributed to each member of the company. Rose-water from a golden or silver *goolabdanee*, is also showered upon the persons of the guests. The signal is then given for the bridegroom and his party to retire to their quarters.

When the marriage ceremony is thus concluded, the parties invited sit down to a banquet. The ladies are first served, and when they have quitted the table, it is relaid for the gentlemen. The Parsees, from their earliest sojourn in India, use only vegetable food on the day of marriage to avoid giving offence to, and out of respect for, the Hindoos, as otherwise a number of animals would require to be killed for a large festive party. The viands, therefore, consist of fish, vegetables, sweetmeats, fruits, preserves, &c. European and native wines are drank very freely, and many toasts proposed to the company. The health of the wedded pair, of their parents, and of the chief men of the assembly, is formally proposed and drunk. But we should be doing great injustice to our countrymen if we omitted to mention that no party ever leaves the table without drinking the health of Her Most Gracious Majesty of England, Queen Victoria, and the Royal family. These toasts are always received with enthusiasm and deafening cheers.

After dinner the ladies retire to their own houses, but the gentlemen sit till a late hour enjoying the pleasures of the nautch that follows. A repetition of the nuptial benediction is also performed by the priests after midnight, but before a few select friends only.

Such are the ceremonies attendant upon a Parsee marriage at the present day, but it may be as well to notice that increased intercourse with Europeans has considerably modified the nature of the festival from what it once was. It has lost in a great measure those purely Eastern features which formerly characterized it; and, although it may consequently be less splendid and showy, it is more in consonance with that enlightenment which Parsees have displayed under Western influence. The long processions, made noisy by horrible ear-splitting native music, the fancifully caparisoned steeds, the boys habited as European officers, and the little girls as English ladies, together with the silver-plated palankeens, and all the semi-barbarous ornaments, have latterly almost entirely disappeared before the effects of increased civilization, which, while giving a more sombre tone to the marriage ceremonials, has imbued them with an infinitely more rational air.

As the married couple are invariably young, separate accommodation is seldom allotted them after their wedding, nor even after they have attained adult age. They live in the same house with the other members of their parents' family. Though a person has six or seven sons, they all reside with their wives and children in the mansion of the sire, and the grey-headed father can often look with pride and pleasure upon the group of children and grandchildren around him. Europeans in Bombay have often witnessed Sir Jamsetjee Jeejeebhoy driving in his spacious open carriage along the public roads in the evening, with half a dozen little ones beside him, and many following him in other carriages. There are, of course, numerous instances where the sons have left their fathers' houses and taken separate quarters for themselves and their wives, and of brothers who, after the death of their parents, have separated from each other. This, however, is not done from any ideas similar to those which prompt Europeans to live separately from their parents after their marriage. Domestic quarrels among the wives of brothers, or with the mother-in-law are generally the causes of the removal.

It is matter of just pride that we find the Parsees have not imitated the barbarous and tyrannical custom of prohibiting widows from remarrying, which is fraught with so much sin and mischief among the Hindoos. The Parsees allow their widows to remarry, and where any are so unfortunate as to lose several husbands, they can enter again into the matrimonial state as often as they desire. Parsee widows, if they marry again, generally do so before they have attained the age of forty; and if one is blessed with children, and is left with sufficient money by her husband to provide for her own and their maintenance, she generally prefers living in celibacy to giving her hand to another.

Bigamy among the Parsees is prohibited except under peculiar circumstances, such as the barrenness of the living wife, or her immoral conduct. The law against bigamy was ever strictly adhered to by the ancient followers of Zurtosht, and by their descendants in India. The Parsee punchayet, who adjudged social and religious disputes among the Parsees, had ever been jealous that this law should not be infringed; and whenever special cases occurred, and parties sought permission to take an additional wife, they reserved the right of deciding as to the validity or otherwise of the grounds on which the application was preferred, and sanctioned or rejected it accordingly.

This practice lasted for centuries after the Parsees had arrived in India, but about the end of the 12th century of the era of Yezdezird, or the beginning of the nineteenth of the Christian era, it was found that the Parsees were gradually infringing the law, and that many an innocent and unoffending wife was forsaken by a vicious husband on trivial grounds, and a new wife taken with impunity. The evil engaged the attention of the punchayet, and they resolved, by every means in their power, to arrest its progress among their countrymen. A public meeting of the Parsee inhabitants of Bombay was convened, by order of the punchayet, in the Dadyshett Fire Temple, where, among other matters relating to the body, certain rules strictly prohibiting bigamy were adopted with the unanimous consent of the assembly. As these rules are not only interesting in themselves, but afford an insight into the special cases under which a person is allowed to take a second wife while the first one is living, we give herewith a literal translation of them :—

"Further, we, the whole punchayet now assembled, have this day resolved that from and after this day no person who has a wife living shall marry another; and if any person feel *compelled* to marry another wife, he shall put his case in writing, and represent the same to the above members of the punchayet; after which the said members will fix a certain time as they shall think proper for the investigation of the case and the hearing of the petition of the complainant, which shall be admitted by the complainant and by all the people; and those who will not admit such decision shall be punished as mentioned below by the punchayet, as to them shall appear fit.

"Further, a person requiring divorce with his first wife, and then permission to marry a second, shall represent his case to the punchayet as above stated; and the punchayet shall meet and inquire into the merits of the case thus brought to their notice; and in case the bad conduct of the first wife be proved according to the usages of our religion, the punchayet shall take securities from him for her alimony (food, clothing, and lodging,) and her jewels, and for funeral expenses on her death, as the punchayet shall deem proper, and then they shall give him permission to take another wife.

"Further, any person having a trifling dispute with his wife shall not be allowed to marry another. In case he shall marry without the permission of the punchayet obtained, as mentioned in the preceding paragraph, he shall be put out of our community.

Further, any person going out of Bombay to take unto himself a wife at Tanna, Carranjah, or at any town or village, while his first wife is alive, shall be turned out of caste by the punchayet on his return to Bombay.

"Further, whoever shall marry a second wife, by permission of the punchayet, the marriage ceremony of such person, if he be a *Shenshoy*, shall be performed by Dustoor Cursetjee Jamsetjee himself, or with his order by priests under him; and if he be a *Kudmee*, by Mulla Firoz, or under his order by priests under him. If any other priests shall perform the ceremony, the punchayet will not acknowledge it, and shall not allow the offending party to enter any Fire Temple; nor shall any person give to priests officiating as above, without permission, donations in funeral and other ceremonies. Any one not acting according to what is above stated, shall be further punished as the punchayet shall think proper.

"Further, any person attending the nuptials of any individual who shall marry a second wife without permission from the punchayet, shall also be punished by the punchayet as they think proper.

"Further, any person having no children, and his wife not passed the age of delivery, shall not marry a second wife, even though he should promise to satisfy his first wife, and obtain her consent to do so. On the other hand, he shall not allow his wife to take unto herself another man for her husband; and the punchayet shall not acknowledge any writing or agreement for the mutual discharge of marriage vows, and shall not allow him to take unto himself another wife, nor the woman to take unto herself another husband; and all who do so without the permission of the punchayet shall be turned out of caste, or shall receive such other punishment as the punchayet shall deem proper.

"Further, any person obtaining permission from the punchayet to take a second wife (his first wife being alive) shall be subject to the payment of such a sum of money for charity, as the punchayet shall deem him able to afford;

and after the payment of such sum, the punchayet may give him permission to marry a second wife."

These rules were passed in March, 1818, and in the June following, one Jemshedjee infringed their conditions by marrying a second wife while his first one was living, and the resolution and justice with which the punchayet of those days punished the offender deserved much praise. Though Jemshedjee was a wealthy person, and connected by relationship with a member of the punchayet, he was not let off easily. He and his father were immediately excommunicated, and only after much solicitation were they re-admitted into the community, and then only on the payment of the proper fine, and undergoing the prescribed ceremonies of purification.* The offender was also compelled to give 2,000 rupees towards the maintenance of his first wife, and to deliver to her all her jewels and ornaments. The severity with which Jemshedjee was punished, deterred others for some time from following his example.

We have now to describe the ceremonies

* He was also compelled, before an assembly of the Parsee community, to beat his own face with his own shoe, for using insulting words to the punchayet.

attending the death of a Parsee. When the medical attendant states that the case is hopeless, the body of the dying man is washed and arrayed in clean clothes. The *dustoor*, or *mobed*, with other priests, repeat sundry texts of the Zend Avasta, the substance of which tends to afford consolation to the dying man, and breathes a prayer on his behalf for the forgiveness of his sins. "May the Almighty pardon you for anything that you may have done against His will, His commandments, and the dictates of the true religion of Zoroaster. May the merciful Lord give you a good and happy abode in the world to which you are about to enter, and may he have mercy on you."

If the dying man be in possession of his senses, he himself joins in these exercises; if not, his son, or nearest relative, or the family priest, bends over him, repeating the words in his ears. When life becomes extinct, the body is wrapped in clean clothes, and placed on an oblong piece of polished stone, which is laid on the floor. The female members and relations of the family then sit down together on a carpet spread in the same room in which the body is placed, the men sitting on benches in the verandah of the house. If death takes place at night, the body is kept in the house till the next morning; but if it happens during the day (four or five hours before sunset), it is removed to its last resting place in the evening.

When the time for the removal of the body approaches, it is placed upon an iron bier, which is brought in by the *nassesalars*, or corpse bearers. This being done, two priests stand facing the corpse, and recite a certain part of the *Izeshne*, a sort of funeral sermon,* containing many solemn and instructive lessons. That human beings are mortal, and must some day or other be called upon to quit this world and enter into the presence of God to give a full account of their doings here, is fully explained. The punishment awaiting the sinner, and the reward in store for those who practice virtue in thought, word, and deed, are fully dilated on. That as riches, wealth, influence, and friends, will have no avail in the next world, the assembly is directed to be heedful how they spend their life in this. That as we do not know at what moment we may be called to give our last account, the duty of being

* The effect of this sermon is lost upon the audience who do not understand the language in which it is delivered.

prepared for death, and of meeting it with resignation and willingness, is fully impressed. That those who desire to reach the eternal paradise in the other world must spend their days in this in holiness and prayers, and in doing good to their fellow creatures. The assembly is forcibly reminded of the day of judgment, when every soul will have to give account. The sermon lasts in this train for about an hour, and is concluded with the words, " May God have mercy on the dead."

The dead body is then taken out of the house to be carried to the *Dokhma*, or Tower of Silence, which is erected in a solitary place, and generally upon a mountain.* The relatives of the departed break into cries and lamentations. The male relatives and friends of the deceased follow the dead body in the funeral procession. Arrived at its resting-place, the iron bier is placed upon the ground, and the face of the dead uncovered for a few minutes, that a last look may be directed upon it, and the whole assembly bow to it.† After a few minutes it is carried by the bearers into

* In Bombay the Dokhmas are built on the most secluded and highest part of the Malabar Hill.

† It is customary among the Parsees, whenever they meet a dead body of their tribe on the road to bow to it, and to remember that the same fate will overtake them sooner or later.

the *Dokhma*, Tower of Silence, and then exposed to the fowls of the air, where it is soon denuded of flesh, and the bones fall through an iron grating into a pit beneath, from which they are afterwards removed into a subterranean entrance made for the purpose.

When the corpse bearers return from the Dokhma, the mobeds, relatives and friends who may have attended the funeral, wash their faces and hands, and jointly offer up prayer to the Almighty to have mercy on the spirit just departed. On the death of a person, his friends, neighbours, and acquaintances visit the relatives of the deceased every morning and evening for three days continuously, to offer consolation to them. On the fourth day a solemn feast takes place, and the relatives go to the Fire Temple, and once more offer prayers for the deceased. The women remain in mourning three, ten, or thirty days, as they may find convenient.

CHAPTER IV.

LAWS AND INTERNAL GOVERNMENT OF THE PARSEES.

The punchayet—Its origin—Progress and decline—A new association established for obtaining civil laws for the Parsees.

The affairs of the Parsee community, after their expatriation from Persia, seem generally to have been managed by a punchayet or committee of five, selected from among their most influential and their wisest men. We have no record of the early history of this body, and are in ignorance as to what laws it was guided by, in its early existence, in the decision of the religious, social, and other disputes arising among the people. The authorities of the place were never called upon to interfere in the matter.

The punchayet was the court of justice, and its decisions, being invariably given after great care and deliberation, were never disputed by the contending parties. Any one refusing to obey the decision of that tribunal was excommunicated from the caste, and his co-religionists held no further intercourse with him. He was not invited to their feasts, religious ceremonies, funeral processions, or marriage festivals. He could not attend the Fire Temples; nor, if he died while in this state of disgrace, could he receive the rites of Parsee burial. Priests were prohibited from performing any religious ceremonies in his family. In fact all intercourse between the party excommunicated and his countrymen was entirely stopped. So great, therefore, was the penalty of excommunication, that the Parsees seldom failed to bow to the decision of their governing body.

This state of affairs seems to have continued until about the middle of the eighteenth century, when the punchayet of Bombay found that they could no longer rule their countrymen so effectively as formerly. Under the old system offenders were punished by being beaten with the shoe; but this mode of punishment it was found almost impossible to enforce when the Parsees were under British rule. The punchayet, therefore, about the year 1778 petitioned the then Governor, William Hornby, requesting legal power to inflict this punishment. The prayer was granted, and the punchayet for the first time, we believe, exercised this power under the sanction of authority.*

About eight years subsequent to this, a violent dispute arose among the *andiaroos*, order of priests, and the *behdins*, or laity, which again rendered Government interference necessary. It arose out of a regulation or ordinance made by the punchayet of Bombay, with the consent of their community, in the year 1777, which prohibited the *behdins* from giving their daughters in marriage to the *andiaroos*. The punchayet took this step in order to counteract an ordinance which the priests had passed among themselves, to the effect that the *andiaroos* should continue to receive in marriage the daughters of the *behdins*, but that they should not bestow their own females upon them. The pun-

* "To the Parsees not of the Priest Caste—

"You are hereby empowered to meet and inquire into all matters that are committed by your caste contrary to what has been agreed to by the majority of the caste, and to punish the offender agreeable to the rules of your caste, so far as not permitting them to come to your feasts, or beat them with shoes, but no other corporeal punishment.

(Signed) "WILLIAM HORNBY."

"*Bombay, 5th July*, 1778."

chayet, therefore, prohibited the giving of daughters in marriage to the priests, and thus sought to deprive them of the unfair advantage they had gained for themselves.

The immediate cause of the quarrel owed its origin to an *andiaroo* contracting his son in marriage to the daughter of a *behdin*, in defiance of the regulations passed by the punchayet. So great was the excitement, that Government was compelled to take notice of the event,* and a committee, composed of three European gentlemen, was appointed to investigate into the causes of the disputes, and to report upon the best mode of bringing about a satisfactory settlement.

After considerable inquiry the commis-

* The following is a true copy of an extract from the minutes of consultation, dated the 21st April 1786:—

"The President acquaints the Board that some religious disputes at present subsist in the caste of Parsees, which he is apprehensive, from the nature and temper of these people, may be attended with disagreeable consequences unless properly settled, and recommends that a committee be appointed to inquire into the rise of these disputes, and to report upon the best mode of finally settling the same. The president at the same time lays before the Board several papers, which have been delivered to him on the occasion by both parties. On consideration of the above, the Board agree to appointment of a committee as proposed by the President, and accordingly Messrs John Forbes, Edward Revenscroft and James Stevens senior, are appointed to form the same."

sioners gave it as their opinion that the *bundobust*, or ordnance, made by the *andiaroos*, was unfair, and fully warranted the *behdins* in withholding their daughters from them. That the resolution passed by the former was calculated to enrich and aggrandise their own caste, and as the *behdins* were excluded from marrying the daughters of the priests, their own women and property were carried into the other caste without any reciprocal advantages being gained by the laity. On these grounds the commissioners observed that the *behdins* had every right to put a stop to this unequal intercourse by the Regulations of 1777.

Before these commissioners the Parsees asserted that the priests made their regulation in their period of power at Surat, while the latter contended that it was the original law of their own religion, and not a modern institution. On this head the commissioners reported that there formerly did exist a mutual intercourse of marriage between the two castes, and the priests themselves were forced to admit that there had been special cases of such marriages. The Commissioners further reported that the Regulation of 1777, which was the immediate cause of the dispute, was equitable in principle, and no blame whatever could with justice be attached to the punchayet, but the fault lay with the priesthood, whose selfishness had necessitated the establishment of some such resolution.

In order to prevent the recurrence of such disputes, and to preserve peace and good order for the future, the commissioners recommended that the punchayet should be formed upon a more equitable basis, and that its authority, which seemed to them to have been rather assumed than conferred, should be defined by, and derived immediately from, Government. In order to effect this, they recommended that some formal instrument should be drawn up which would have the effect of giving more weight and efficacy to the decisions of the punchayet. They further advised that the punchayet, so constituted, should have powers given to it for settling petty disputes and matters of religious forms and ceremonies. But they likewise gave it as their opinion that the power of punishing by the shoe, which the punchayet exercised, was objectionable, and recommended that it should be withdrawn.

With the general tenor of this report the Governor in Council concurred. It was decided that the punchayet, or general assembly of the Parsees, had a right to make regulations for the general benefit and good of the Parsee people, as is customary with the tribes of every denomination living under the protection of the British Government.

In conformity with the recommendation of the committee, the Governor in Council directed the punchayet, to return the names of twenty-four persons, from whom twelve could be selected as a committee for the management of the affairs of the Parsees and the settlement of their private disputes. It was hoped that a committee thus appointed would be the means of putting a stop to further dissension in the body.

The names of twenty-four gentlemen having been sent in, twelve* (six of whom were priests and six laymen) were appointed by Government, under date the 1st of January, 1787, for the purposes above mentioned, and enjoined to do "strict justice to all parties without

* The twelve appointed were, Jamsetjee Bhooga Mody, Nanabhoy Byramjee, Manackjee Nourojee Wadia, Dadabhoy Nasserwanjee, Heerjee Jewanjee, Sorabjee Muncherjee, Sapoorjee Bomonjee, Dustoor Cowasjee Rustomjee, Sorabjee Nanabhoy Sett, Dorabjee Framjee, Cowasjee Bhicajee, Dorabjee Furdoonjee.

fear, favour, or affection to any one." The decisions of a body thus expressly sanctioned by Government had great influence and weight with the majority of the Parsees, and its decrees were respected and obeyed.

But this hopeful state of affairs was not of long duration; before the end of the eighteenth century the punchayet was again powerless. Death had considerably thinned the numbers of the committee originally appointed by Government, and proper steps had not been taken to fill the vacancies as they arose. The sons of the old members assumed a seat in the body, and, as is usual in such cases, their authority was estimated at its proper worth.

On the great Parsee gathering of the 4th March, 1818, when certain rules were framed against the practice of bigamy, the punchayet candidly confessed its own weakness, and duly proceeded to elect a fresh council, consisting of eighteen* members, of whom twelve were

* The members of this second council were, Davar Framjee Nanabhoy, Wadiajee Nourojee Jamshedjee, Sett Cursetjee, Ardasurjee, Dhunjeebhoy Sorabjee Ready Money, Wadiajee Hormisjee Bomonjee, Framjee Cowasjee Bunajee, Sorabjee Vacha Ghandy, Burjorjee Dorabjee Dady Burjorna, Cursetjee Manackjee Shroff, Dadabhoy Cowasjee Sayerna, Pestonjee

laymen and six priests. The punchayet, thus resuscitated, was respected for a time, but unfortunately it again fell into contempt.

In the year 1838, backed by almost all the wealthy and respectable part of the community, the punchayet again made an effort to derive formal power directly from the Legislative Council of India. They also sent to that Assembly, through the Bombay Government, certain questions and answers embracing the rights of inheritance among their own people, with a request that, upon the basis of those answers, a law regulating the same might be framed.

In their petition to the Legislative Council, the Parsees, with a view to obtain power for the punchayet, thus expressed themselves:— "If, as we hope, your Lordship and the Legislative Council of India may be graciously pleased to pass a regulation in conformity with our desires, the next point to be considered is the enforcement of such regulation. The punchayet, we regret to inform your Lordship, is now almost powerless, either for good or

Beramjee Pandena, Nourojee Meherjee, Dustoor Cursetjee Jamsetjee of Nowsaree, Moolla Ferooz ben Kavusjee, Merwanjee Nourojee Sett, Sett Rustomjee Sapoori, Dorabjee Framjee Punthekee, and Hormusjee Dorabjee Laskaree.

evil; and unless that body is made respected by the act of Government, the most serious consequences must ensue to the best interests of our caste. So long as the caste continued limited in number, and willing to obey the decisions of the punchayet, the want of recognised authority in that body did not appear so forcibly as it now does to the feelings and understandings of those interested in the welfare and prosperity of the Parsee nation. Of late, however, a new spirit has sprung up, and each man claims a right of acting as he may think fit, and very often in defiance of the decisions of the punchayet, and in wilful opposition both to the spirit and letter of our laws and usages. To be useful and of avail, both the law, and those who administer it, must be respected; and respect in ignorant minds seldom exists without some portion of fear. The lower orders of Parsees see that the punchayet has no power to punish, and, therefore, do not respect its authority or its decisions; and as it has hitherto been our pride, and almost the wonder of surrounding people, that so large a body as the Parsees now comprise, should be self-governed, we are led thus most urgently to pray that your Lordship will invest the punchayet with an efficient authority to control the vicious and encourage the virtuous."

Before the memorial was transmitted to the Supreme Government, it was referred by the local authorities to the Judges of the Supreme Court of Judicature at Bombay, and the opinion they expressed was unfavourable to the creation of the authority solicited by the punchayet. They wrote:—

"We concur in their (petitioners') wishes in regard to the punchayet so far as to think it highly desirable that there should exist a tribunal satisfactory to themselves, and authorized to decide matrimonial and some other questions where Parsees only were parties to them. But we fear the difficulties are much greater than they apprehend. If its authority were compulsory, questions might arise as to the legality and regularity of proceedings before it; besides that, no longer depending for their force on general consent, its decisions would be much less likely, in the absence of any authentic standard of law, to give general satisfaction.

"But we conceive the inevitable consequence would be, that, unless they had a lawyer as an assessor, which probably they would by no means desire, the Parsee community would be greatly harassed by collision between that Court and the Supreme Court. If once its jurisdiction were established, its exercise in proper cases would be a matter of right which must, if withheld, be enforced by a writ of mandamus from the Queen's Court. If the limits of its jurisdiction, which it would be most difficult accurately to define, and the definition of which would with great difficulty be applied (particularly by persons of totally different habits of thinking) to particular cases as they occurred, were exceeded, writs of prohibition would be the necessary consequence.

"From the Reformation to the eighteenth century, in the course of which period most of the chief questions have been settled, our books are full of collisions of this kind between the spiritual and temporal courts in England. But it is manifest that they would be more frequent and more harassing here. We are very sensible of the value of that highly respectable body the Parsee punchayet, but we fear that a total change of its character from an assembly qualified to administrate a liberal system of arbitration to one cramped on every side in its operations by the necessity of administering, with the rigour of law, a system (if it amount to one) only calculated to guide the discretion of arbitrators, must be the result of giving it coercive authority."

This opinion of her Majesty's Judges was fatal to the petition; and from that time until the present, all hope of obtaining a Government sanction for the punchayet has been abandoned. Thus disappointed, that body tried to assume the power over the people which was refused them by the authorities; and, as a matter of course, they failed.

The members of the punchayet did not, however, seem to feel the humiliating position in which they were placed, but continued not only to assume the name of a punchayet, but fruitlessly attempted to carry on the functions of that body.

For the last fifteen or twenty years, the body known among the Parsees as the punchayet, has not possessed the slightest influence over the people. It has occasionally exhibited some signs of vitality, but never in the right direction. Its orders, if it ever dare issue any, are unheeded or disobeyed. Excommunication from caste, a sentence which the Parsees of old so greatly dreaded, is not only unheeded, but ridiculed, as the party excommunicated is sure to possess the sympathy and intercourse of his friends in the teeth of the order of the punchayet.

It is not to be imagined that this state of feeling arises from a riotous community. The decisions of the present punchayet, while they are neither consistent nor impartial, are not in accordance with justice, and the consequence is, that the body is as destitute of moral weight as of legal power. When a friend or relative of any member of the punchayet, or, indeed, any person of wealth or influence, commits an offence against his caste people, he is not only screened, but justified. While, if the offender be a poor man, the punchayet steps forward, with all the severity which characterized its rule of old, to make him an example to others.

Common sense suggests that a body professing to do justice with one law for the rich and another for the poor cannot command any moral respect whatever. Its shameless partiality, some time since, drew forth from one of its oldest and most respectable members an ugly exposure of the acts of his colleagues perfectly fatal to their respectability. This memorable protest was the work of the late

Framjee Cowasjee, Esquire,* a name still revered by the whole Parsee community. The punchayet was thus virtually extinguished, and our worthy baronet, Sir Jamsetjee Jeejeebhoy, publicly acknowledged this fifteen years since.† It is now powerless either for good or evil, and performs no other functions than those of trustees to certain charitable

* The following is a short abstract of Framjee's minute, from a literal translation of it published in an English newspaper some years ago. The minute was addressed to the members of the punchayet, and it fully exposes the extent to which corruptions had reached the Parsee community, and the utter apathy and carelessness with which the punchayet overlooked the unhappy state of things. "I have resolved," says Framjee, "that I shall not hereafter join with you in transacting any of the punchayet's business. Individuals calling themselves Zoroastrians have now become so reckless, that they look upon bigamy and other monstrous sins as anything but sinful. I can cite numberless instances of persons in this place, who have not only deserted their lawful wives and joined in matrimony with others, in defiance of the rules of our community, as also of many who are recklessly living and spending their existence in the houses of unprincipled women. You, who call yourselves members of the punchayet, will not only take no notice of these affairs, but allow such sinful persons to participate in all the rights of Zoroastrianism. You will not bring such offenders to punishment, but on the contrary, sometimes think very lightly of their offences. It cannot be said that you are not cognizant of this growing evil, and if you do not discharge your trust faithfully, what answer will you give to your Maker on the Day of Judgment?"

† See Kholasa-i-Punchayet, edited by Sir Jamsetjee.

funds. The word punchayet, therefore, now applied to the body, is a misnomer.

We conclude this chapter with some notice of the laws by which the Parsees are guided in the distribution of their property, and which regulate the rights of inheritance among them. The Parsees in India seem never to have possessed the code of laws which their prophets had devised for them. It is said to have been lost with their other religious books on their expatriation. In their early sojourn in India, they probably depended upon ordinary and recognised principles of justice and equity, and if any dispute arose regarding succession to property, or rights of inheritance, their punchayet gave a final decision.

It is evident, however, that the ancient usage was to divide equally among all the children the whole of the property, whether personal or landed, of an intestate person, and this course having been followed from generation to generation, became common law in the community. No questions were ever raised respecting the rights of dividing landed property by will.

So long as they agreed among themselves, and kept their disputes from being taken into the authorized courts of justice, this usage was strictly adhered to. But when litigious fellows discovered that disputes regarding inheritance and succession might be determined according to English law by the authorised court of the country (no provision having been made in the charter of that court for the regulation of such disputes among them, as was provided for the Hindoos and Mahomedans) a new spirit arose among them. Many elder sons whose fathers had died intestate, threatened, in violation of long observed usage, to take the whole of the freehold property to themselves, to the prejudice of their brothers, as they knew that the English law being on their side, the court would decide in their favour. This created much excitement among the Parsees, who lost no time in forwarding a memorial to the Legislative Council, in which they clearly pointed out the mischief that would be occasioned by the application of English law to themselves in the above matter.

The petition had its due weight with that assembly, and on the 15th of May 1837, an Act * was passed by the Governor-General

* Act No. IX of 1837 :—

I. It is hereby enacted, that from the 1st day of June, 1837, all immoveable property situate within the jurisdiction of any of the Courts established by His Majesty's Charter, shall, as far as regards the transmission of such property on the death and of India in Council, which declared that "real property within the jurisdiction of the Supreme Court shall, as regards its transmission by the will of a Parsee testator, or on the death of a Parsee intestate, be taken to be, and to have always been, of the nature of chattels real." The dispute in this matter was thus finally settled. But the application of English law in various other civil disputes has been productive of much inconvenience as well as misery among the Parsees.

As the litigious propensities of the people began to increase, and the punchayet lost its power, the want of a regular recognised code

intestacy of any Parsee having a beneficial interest in the same, or by last will of any such Parsee, be taken to be and to have been of the nature of chattels real, and not of freehold.

II. Provided always that in any suit at law or in equity, which shall be brought for the recovery of such immoveable property as is aforesaid, no advantage shall be taken of any defect of title arising out of the transmission of such property upon the death and intestacy of any Parsee having a beneficial interest in the same, or by the last will of any such Parsee, if such transmission took place before the said 1st day of June, 1837, and if such transmission were, either according to the rules which regulate the transmission of freehold property, or else took place with the acquiescence of all persons to whom any interest in that property would, according to the rules which regulate the transmission of chattels real, have accrued upon the death of such Parsee.

W. H. Macnaghten,
Secretary to Government of India.

of laws among the Parsees was keenly felt. The British Government, true to its pledge, administers justice impartially to each class of the community, according to its own customs and rules. Disputes among the Hindoos and Mahomedans, are decided according to the sacred books of those people as interpreted by their Shastrees and Kazees.

The case of the Parsees is unhappily different. The few sacred books that they now possess do not contain much to guide the judges in their civil disputes. In the absence of such information, an English judge finds it extremely difficult to ascertain with certainty what the rules and customs of the people are. The Judges, who have within the last twenty years presided over Her Majesty's Supreme Court at Bombay, have frequently suggested to the Parsees to remedy this evil by preparing a code of laws, which, if agreed upon by the mass of their people, would be accepted as law in the English Courts of Justice.

Acting upon such advice, two or three efforts were made to devise a code for the Parsees, but they proved unsuccessful, owing to a want of unanimity among the people. The last step, however, which the Parsee community has taken in this matter, aided by the wisdom and experience of the elders, and the vigour, activity, and industry of their educated and younger members, is likely to meet with better success.

In pursuance of advertisements which appeared in all the Guzerati Journals, a public meeting of the members of this community was held on the 20th August, 1855, in the hall of one of their fire-temples, for the purpose of adopting measures for declaring the laws binding upon the professors of the Zoroastrian Faith. There were present on the occasion, besides the heads of the community, many of its most influential members. The whole assemblage numbered upwards of 3,000 persons.

The object of the meeting was so fully explained by one of the speakers, that we are tempted to give here an English translation of his speech entire. It not only furnishes a full account of the previous efforts to obtain the object, but shows the great necessity of such an enactment for the Parsees as they are now seeking. The following is the address:

"At the time when India became subject to the beneficent and constitutional sway of the British, the Government gave a pledge and guarantee to the people of this extensive country, that all civil cases in which Hindoos and Mahomedans were concerned would be decided according to Hindoo and Mahomedan law. That the enjoyment of those rights and privileges which they have possessed from their ancestors, will be secured to them in all English Courts. From the time the country came into the hands of the English, about two centuries ago, to the present moment, the British Government have performed their promise, and the customs and usages of the Hindoos and Mahomedans have been respected by them in all matters bearing upon their civil rights, and in consequence, they have been able to enjoy the benefit of such rights.

"It is to be regretted, that members of the Zoroastrian community who live in this country under the British rule, are not in a position to enjoy, in the administration of justice, the same privileges with respect to their ancestral customs and usages, and the British authorities and the Courts of Justice have not up to this time recognised any of their laws.

"It is our bounden duty to endeavour to obviate the evils that from time to time arise from the want of such fixed laws applicable to our people, as would be recognised and enforced by British authorities and judges, and from application of the English, Hindoo, or other laws, in the adjudication of those cases in which Zoroastrians are concerned. It appears from an English pamphlet relating to the Parsee laws, published in 1843, that during the years 1836, 1837, and 1838, most of the leading members of the Parsee community endeavoured to procure such legislative enactments as seemed to them necessary. All cases involving questions of inheritance, conjugal rights and disputes among the Parsees, are decided by the Supreme Court according to English law, and not according to Parsee customs and usages; hence the evils and disadvantages from which we suffer.

"In 1835, a Parsee filed a suit in the Supreme Court here, claiming, as eldest son, the whole of the landed property of his father, who died intestate. This step created a great sensation among the Parsees, who petitioned the Legislative Council, through the Bombay Government, praying for an act for the Parsee community for preventing the eldest son from inheriting the whole of his father's freehold estate, and declaring such property to be personal property, divisible among all the heirs of the Parsee according to their usage. The Legislative Council at once acceded to this prayer, and in the month of May, 1837, an act was passed to that effect. Mr. Borradaile, on behalf of the Government, had put several questions to the Parsee community of Surat regarding their laws of inheritance, but that body not having replied to them, the leading members of the Parsee punchayet of Bombay published those questions in the form of a pamphlet in the year 1832, and solicited answers from the Parsee community, but this invitation was likewise unsuccessful.

"In 1836, however, the members of the Parsee punchayet and other Zoroastrians having framed answers to those questions submitted them, in 1838, through the local Government to the Legislative Council, with a petition praying for an enactment for regulating the laws of inheritance among the Parsees according to their ancestral customs. But owing to another petition having been transmitted to the Legislative Council by some of the Zoroastrians, embodying adverse opinions, and owing to several other causes, the object was not gained.

"In 1841 Mr. Borradaile was again applied to, but owing to want of unanimity among our community, and other obstacles, the matter was neglected and dropped altogether. The judges of the Supreme Court have at various times suggested to our countrymen the propriety and advisability of procuring an enactment on the subject of their laws of inheritance, marriage, and divorce, which enactment would obviate the difficulties now experienced in cases that come before the court involving such questions, and would promote domestic peace and happiness, and secure to the Parsees the observance of their ancient customs and usages.

"Sir Erskine Perry, our late Chief Justice, and a well-wisher to the natives, wrote thus to a well-known member of the Parsee community in 1843, 'I have been so fully impressed for some time past with the necessity of a legislative enactment for the Parsees, that I had determined to draw up a report to Government, pointing out what the subjects are on which legislation is required, and discussing the different provisions which it might be expedient to adopt.' It is well known to all that this intelligent, experienced, and clever jurist repeatedly expressed his earnest desire and willingness to assist us in procuring laws for our guidance.

"Now it is the duty of the Parsees to make a combined effort to procure suitable and requisite laws framed for the Zoroastrian community, and without showing any sign of indolence or tardiness, to deliberate and make such arrangements, and adopt such measures as will ensure to us the fulfilment of our object. Their exertions will not remain unappreciated, and they will have the proud satisfaction of seeing their labours, through Divine favour, crowned with success.

"Mr. Le Geyt, our well-wisher, who is conversant with the customs and feelings of the Parsees, and who now fills the honourable post of member for Bombay of the Legislative Council of India, will, we trust, exert his utmost to obtain for us the enactment of suitable and requisite laws. It is our hope that our local judges will also assist us in this undertaking.

"Those of our countrymen who are subject to the jurisdiction of the Supreme Court of Bombay are at present subjected to English law, and are debarred from the benefit of their ancestral usages; the ruin entailed on the Parsees by that English law which awards all freehold property to the eldest son of all intestate property, to the exclusion of the other heirs, has been remedied by Act IX. of 1857. Nevertheless, the property of a Zoroastrian who dies without having made a will, is still liable to be divided according to the English law, and it is therefore the duty of all Zoroastrians to provide a proper remedy.

"Our people have to suffer much injury and disadvantage, owing to our not possessing a regular code of laws recognised by the authorities; and, furthermore, the judges experience inconvenience and difficulty in deciding cases relating to the Parsees, and sometimes they are unable to arrive at a satisfactory conclusion. They have, therefore, frequently recommended to the leading members of our caste the advisability of preparing, after mature deliberation, a draft of laws, with a view to get them sanctioned by Government.

"So far back as the year 1827, Mr. Borrodaile, Registrar of the Sudder Adawlut, addressed a letter, at the recommendation of Government, to Mody Rushtomjee Khurshedjee and the Parsee community of Surat, which is of such importance that I take leave to read to the meeting the first three paragraphs.

"'First. It appears, from observing your customs and usages since the time of Governor Duncan, that you do not possess a regular code of laws, to which all the men of your nation pay obedience. In consequence of this a great many disputes arise amongst you, to the great detriment of your people.

"'Second. It would not have been deemed necessary to ask you to frame a code if you had an ancient book of laws or tradition which the whole of your tribe accept; but, on inquiry, it appears that amongst your books there is no such work. From mature consideration, and an attentive observance of your present manners and customs, it appears that some of your usages are founded on the laws recorded in your books, while a great many are based on your ancient immemorial customs that prevailed amongst your ancestors, while some of your tribe at present follow no laws, and act in any way they please. At present there is no record of your ancient usages. It is therefore the opinion of Government that you should assemble and consult together, and with your unanimous consent commit these laws and customs to writing; and, after holding mature deliberations, adopt a code of laws for your government and guidance, otherwise there will be no end to disputes and litigation amongst the body of your nation. I have, by the order of Government, prepared and transmitted to you a series of questions on the subject of your laws, which you are desired to take into your serious consideration, and after deliberating on the subject, forward explicit answers to them, such as you all unanimously agree to and approve.

"'Third. After unanimously adopting such laws in the manner aforesaid, should it be thought necessary to amend, alter, erase, or add any clauses therein, you are at liberty to do so with the unanimous consent of all the men of your nation. It is therefore advisable that you should desire the welfare and prosperity, of your tribe, and of your posterity, and after deliberating on this important subject, you should, with one voice, frame answers to the questions herewith forwarded to you for your attentive consideration, and return the same to Government. All cases, actions, and suits will be decided by Government functionaries in conformity to the laws approved, agreed upon, and transmitted by the unanimous consent of your nation.'

"It is the duty of our countrymen, the Parsees, to adopt the important recommendation contained in the letter of Mr. Borrodaile I have just quoted, and to prepare a draft of suitable and appropriate laws, and to adopt measures for the purpose of procuring an enactment from the Legislative Council in India.

"If such laws were passed, all disputes and differences between the members of our community would be decided according to the customs and usages of our ancestors, and not in accordance to English laws and usages. Thus the peace and prosperity of our people will be enhanced, and the rich and poor will derive the same benefit, namely, that of a fixed and uniform code of laws; all of us will succeed in obtaining substantial justice in conformity to our immemorial usages; and disputes and quarrels which frequently take place between mother and children, brother and sister, husband and wife, will greatly diminish, and every one will know exactly what his rights are, and act on such knowledge. If the leading and other members of our community unite, co-operate, and zealously exert themselves in the noble cause of procuring a legislative enactment adapted to our nation, this object will, through the grace of God, be accomplished."

The meeting having resolved that it was deeply impressed with the necessity of procuring for their community the enactment of laws adapted to their race, and such as might be recognised and enforced by the local authorities and by courts of justice, a managing committee of one hundred and fifty gentlemen was appointed. These again selected by ballot from among themselves twenty to form a sub-committee, to which was entrusted the task of framing a draft of the requisite provisions.

After considerable inquiries and investigation into the manners, customs, and religion of the Parsees, a draft Act has been prepared by this body, and there is little doubt that it will finally be adopted by the whole community. We have been fortunate enough to obtain a copy of it, and conclude this chapter by annexing an English translation of the document, as a perusal of it will afford the best index to the social customs of the Parsees, and an insight into the advanced spirit of these people from the liberal views it exposes.

WHEREAS doubts have arisen as to the laws to be administered with regard to the succession and inheritance to the estates of deceased Parsees; and whereas it is expedient that one uniform and settled law on the subject should prevail throughout India, having reference to, and incorporating as far as is consistent with sound principles of legislation, the usages and customs which hitherto have prevailed among the Parsees, and been authorised by their sacred writings: Be it enacted as follows:—

I. That from and after the passing of this Act, every Parsee, whether male or female, single or married, who shall have attained the age of twenty-one years, shall be entitled by will to dispose of any property whether real or personal, ancestral or acquired, of which he or she may die possessed, to such person or persons as he or she thinks fit:—and that for this purpose a married woman with regard to her own property, howsoever acquired, shall be treated and considered as a *feme sole.*

II. Such will in order to be valid must be in writing, and executed in a manner hereinafter mentioned (that is to say) it shall be signed at the foot or end thereof bý the testator or testatrix, or by some other person in his or her presence, and by his or her direction, and such signature shall be made or acknowledged by the testator or testatrix as the signature to his or her will or codicil, in the presence of two or more witnesses present at the same time, and such witnesses shall subscribe the will in the presence of the testator or testatrix; but no form of attestation shall be necessary.

III. That after the payment of debts, funeral expenses, and just expenses of every sort, the clear residue of the property, whether real or personal, ancestral or acquired, of any Parsee dying intestate, shall be distributed in manner following:—

To the widow or widower, one share.
To the sons one share each.
To the daughters, half a share each.

IV. If any child of the intestate shall have died in his or her lifetime, the widow and issue of such child shall be entitled in the proportions hereinbefore mentioned in section iii., set forth to such share of the property of the intestate to which such child would have been entitled, had he or she survived the intestate; but if there shall be no issue, the widow shall be entitled to one fourth only of such share as aforesaid. Provided always that the widow of such child shall not have contracted a second marriage at the time of the death of the said intestate, in which case such widow shall not be entitled to any portion of such property, but the same shall be distributed as if such widow were also deceased.

V. That a son duly adopted in the manner pointed out in

section xii. to xviii. shall be entitled to, and shall take the same share of any intestates, as a natural born son is entitled to by virtue of the preceding sections.

VI. If the intestate leave no lineal descendants, nor any adopted son, his or her father and mother shall take one moiety of the estate, in equal shares if they both be living, and his or her widow or widower the other moiety. If there be no father or mother, his or her father's relatives, in the order in the table hereinafter specified, shall take one moiety, and the other shall go to the widow or widower. If there be no relatives on the father's side, the widow or widower shall take the whole.

VII. If the intestate leaves neither widow nor widower, nor issue, nor any adopted son, his or her next of kin, in the order set forth in the following table, shall be entitled to succeed to the whole of his or her property, whether real or personal, ancestral or acquired. The next of kin standing first in the table shall always have preference over those standing second, the second to the third, and so on in succession, subject to the condition that each female shall receive half the portion of each male, standing in the same degree of propinquity.

1. Father and mother.
2. Brothers and sisters, (father's side, and the widows and issue of any deceased brother or sister subject to the rules and in the proportions hereinbefore set forth.
3. Nephews and nieces by the father's side, and the widow and issue of any deceased nephew or niece in the proportions and subject to rules hereinbefore set forth.
4. Paternal grandfather and paternal grandmother.
5. Children of the paternal grandfather.
6. Grandchildren of the paternal grandfather, or in failure of these their lineal descendants.
7. Great grandfather and great grandmother, paternal.
8. Children of the great grandfather, paternal.
9. Grandchildren of great grandfather paternal, or in failure of these their lineal descendants.
10. Brothers and sisters, by the mother's side, and the widows and issue of any deceased brother or sister by

the mother's side, subject to the rules and in the proportions hereinbefore set forth.

11. Nephews and nieces by the mother's side and the widows and issue of any deceased nephew or niece, in the proportions and subject to rules hereinbefore set forth.
12. Maternal grandfather and grandmother.
13. Children of maternal grandfather.
14. Grandchildren of maternal grandfather, or in failure of these, their lineal descendants.
15. Son's widow (if she has not contracted a second marriage at the death of the intestate).
16. Daughters-in-law of the father (if they have not contracted a second marriage at the death of the intestate.)
17. Daughters-in-law of the paternal grandfather (if they have not contracted a second marriage at the death of the intestate.)
18. Daughters-in-law of maternal grandfather (if they have not contracted a second marriage at the death of the intestate.)
19. Husband of the intestate's deceased daughter.
20. Children of the intestate's father-in-law (father of his last wife if more than one), or in failure of these, their lineal descendants.
21. Widows of brothers-in-law of the intestate (brothers of his last wife if more than one.)
22. Father and mother of maternal grandfather.
23. Children of maternal grandfather.
24. Grandchildren of maternal great grandfather, or in failure of these, their lineal descendants.
25. Children of paternal grandmother's father, or in failure of these, their lineal descendants.

And whereas doubts have arisen as to the rights of married women over property given or bequeathed to them after betrothal or during marriage.

VIII. Be it enacted, that all property of whatever kind soever, which shall be given, granted, conveyed, or bequeathed to, or which shall in any way be acquired by any woman, whether married or single, shall unless the same shall be otherwise expressed by the writing or deed, granting or conveying, assigning or bequeathing the same, be and be taken to be her sole and separate property, and she shall have and exercise the same absolute control over the disposal and use thereof, notwithstanding any marriage which she may contract, and may enter into any contracts relating to the disposition and use thereof, and give as effectual acquittances and receipts in respect thereto, and sue and be sued in any action or suit in respect thereof or touching the same as if she were a *feme sole*.

IX. That no husband shall be held liable for any debt contracted by his wife, unless contracted by his express or implied authority. Provided that nothing herein contained, shall be construed to exempt the husband from his liability to provide for his wife suitable maintenance and necessaries.

X. The illegitimate child of any intestate shall be entitled to be maintained out of his or her estate until such child shall have attained twenty-one years but no longer.

XI. The widow or widower, sons or adopted son and daughters, or lineal descendants of a bastard dying intestate, shall inherit his or her property in the several proportions hereinbefore specified, in the same manner as if he or she had been born in lawful wedlock.

XII. If any man above the age of fourteen years and three months have no son nor any male lineal descendant, and if he shall have adopted in his lifetime any person, whether he be his blood relation or not, as his son by his last will, or by a written instrument duly executed and attested by two witnesses, the person so adopted shall be treated and shall have the same rights as his lawfully begotten son, and if the adopted die intestate, such adopted son shall inherit the property of the deceased, in the same manner as if he were his own lawful son.

XIII. If a man having adopted a son authorised in section xii., should subsequently have a son born to him in lawful wedlock, the adoption shall be null and void. In case a son be not born, no one except the adoptive father has the right of cancelling or annulling the adoption.

XIV. If a person die intestate, leaving neither a son nor any male lineal descendants, and if he in his lifetime has not adopted a son, as authorised by section xii., any one of his under-mentioned nearest of kin, in the order hereinafter set forth, shall have the right of being adopted as a son of the deceased; iand if the person, having such right, consent in his own name, f of legal age, or by guardian if a minor, to be adopted as the son of the deceased, the party so consenting shall be held to be the son and heir of the deceased, in the same manner as if he were the lawfully begotten son of the deceased.

1. The son either of the brother or paternal uncle of the deceased, if betrothed or married to the surviving daughter of the deceased at or before the time of his death, shall have the right to be adopted. If more daughters than one are in this category, the right of precedence shall be claimed by the husband of the eldest daughter; in case of failure or refusal, the sons (according to the priority of birth) of the eldest daughter of the deceased, if married to a lineal descendant of the paternal grandfather or great-grandfather shall be eligible, in default of these, or if they refuse to be adopted.
2. The brothers of the deceased in the order of their birth, in case of defect or refusal.
3. The sons of the eldest brother (in the order of their birth. In case of defect or refusal of these, the sons of the next brother in like manner shall be eligible and so on. In failure of these or in case of a refusal
4. The eldest son of the eldest paternal uncle by the father's side. In case of defect or refusal, the other sons of the other paternal uncles, in like manner, shall be eligible; or in failure of these, or in the event of their not consenting
5. The sons of the eldest daughter in the order of their birth, and failing these, the sons of the next daughter in like manner.
6. The sons of the eldest sister in the order of seniority; and failing these, the sons of the next sister in like manner.

XV. If any person, either by his will, or by any writing executed in the presence of two attesting witnesses, delegate to another the power of adoption to take effect after his death, the person so adopted by virtue of such power, shall, agreeably to section xii., be held to be the son and heir of the deceased, in the same manner as if he were his own legitimate son.

XVI. If a person die intestate, and if he have neither a son nor male lineal descendant, and if none of the relatives and connections mentioned in section xiv. be available for the purpose of adoption, the widow of the deceased, or in case of defect or refusal, his daughters in the order of their birth, or in default of these, or in case they decline, the nearest of kin of the deceased in the order prescribed in section vii., shall have the power to adopt a son to the deceased, provided such adoption take place in the presence of at least three witnesses, on or before the morning of the fourth day after the death of the deceased; and if the person so adopted be of legal age and consent to be adopted, or if a minor consent through his guardian to such adoption, he shall be deemed to be the son and the heir of the intestate, as if he were a lawfully begotten son of the deceased. But if the intestate die in a foreign country a son shall be adopted to him as aforesaid within the period of four days after the receipt of the intelligence of his death. If the person so nominated subsequently decline the nomination another person might be appointed at any subsequent period.

XVII. Any person who does not profess the Zoroastrian religion, or who is a lunatic, or who shall at the death of the intestate be undergoing sentence of transportation, shall be deemed disqualified for the duties of such adopted son, and the person who next to him has a right to be adopted, as directed in sections xiv. and xvi., shall be nominated in his place, and shall be entitled to all the privileges of an adopted son of the deceased.

XVIII. Any person adopted as a son of a deceased Parsee in conformity to sections xii., xiv., xvi., and xvii., cannot again be adopted as a son to another deceased Parsee.

XIX. If a person die without leaving a will, letters of

administration of the property of the intestate shall be granted to the undermentioned relatives successively in the following order. If such relatives refuse to take out letters of administration, or if they be not of a legal age or be otherwise disqualified, letters of administration shall be granted to the person standing next in order. And if there shall be no person standing in such a degree of relationship to the intestate, then to such other fit and proper person as to the court shall seem meet.

1. Widow or widower and sons.
2. Son's son.
3. Daughters.
4. Father.
5. Mother.
6. Daughters of son.
7. Sons of daughters.
8. Daughters of daughters.
9. Brother.
10. Sisters.
11. Uncles by the father's side.
12. Widow of the deceased son if she has not contracted a second marriage at the death of the intestate.

XX. If a testator at his death has not appointed an executor of his last will and testament, or if the person so appointed refuse to act, in either of which cases administration shall be granted to the persons mentioned in section xix.

XXI. A Parsee shall be deemed to have attained his or her majority at the age of twenty-one years, and shall thenceforth be competent to make contracts, to claim the free use of his or her property, to act as guardian, executor, or administrator, and to dispose of his or her property by will. And whereas it is desirable to ascertain the law and define the rights and the relative positions of parent and child and guardian and ward.

XXII. Be it further enacted, That the father shall be entitled to the custody of his children, whether legitimate or illegitimate, and the guardianship of their estates until they attain the age of twenty-one years, provided he be not by lunacy or other cause disqualified for the due discharge of his duties and and the exercise of his rights towards such child. And he may appoint one or more guardians by will duly executed. And upon his death, in the absence of any such appointments, the mother, or in case of her death or disqualification, the other relatives of the child, in the order mentioned in section vii., shall be appointed guardian, and shall possess all the rights and privileges of the father, except as hereinafter is provided.

XXIII. Where any dispute shall arise between the father and mother of any child under the age of six years, the personal custody of the child shall belong to the mother until the child shall have attained its full age of six years.

XXIV. Any betrothal or marriage contracted by a child under the age of twenty-one years without the consent of the father, or if the father be dead or disqualified as aforesaid, of the mother, shall be considered null and void. And every betrothal or contract of marriage made by the parents on behalf of a child above the age of sixteen years, shall not be binding on the child if made without obtaining his or her consent. In case the father and mother be both dead or disqualified, the right of granting or withholding consent to betrothal or marriage shall be vested in the guardian, but in such case shall wholly cease and determine on the child attaining the age of sixteen years.

XXV. The right of the mother, upon the death or disqualification of the father as aforesaid, to the custody and guardianship of the child shall cease altogether on her re-marriage, except where the child shall be under the age of six years, in which case the personal custody of the child shall remain with the mother, notwithstanding her re-marriage, until such child shall have attained the age of six years; and the guardianship shall, on such attainment by the child of the age of six years, be vested in and exercised by the paternal grandfather, brother, maternal uncle, or paternal grandmother of the child, in the order set forth in the following section. But, if all these relatives be dead, disqualified, or unwilling to act, the right of the mother shall revert to her notwithstanding such re-marriage.

XXVI. Upon the death or disqualification as aforesaid of the father and mother, and the non-appointment of any testamentary guardian, the undermentioned surviving relatives, according to the following order, shall be entitled to the custody and guardianship of the person and property of the child; provided they are not by lunacy, difference of religion, or other just cause, disqualified for so acting.

1. Grandfather, paternal.
2. Brothers, in the order of seniority.
3. Uncles by the father's side, in the order of seniority.
4. Grandmother, paternal.
5. Sisters, in the order of seniority.
6. Sons of the uncle by the father's side, in the order of seniority.
7. Grandfather, paternal.
8. Grandfather, maternal.
9. Uncles by the mother's side, in the order of seniority.
10. Father's sisters, in the order of seniority.
11. Mother's sisters, in the order of seniority.
12. Any relative or suitable person who may be desirous of being appointed.

XXVII. In constructing this Act the relationship, if not otherwise expressed, is to be traced through the male line only, and brethren of the half-blood by the mother's side are not in any case to be entitled to succeed unless expressly named.

CHAPTER V.

COMMERCIAL PURSUITS.

Early occupations of the Parsees in India—British power exceedingly favourable to their interest and the development of their commercial and enterprising spirit—Extensive commercial intercourse at the present day—A remarkable instance of industry and a love for the extension of agriculture—Testimony to their general intelligence and enterprise—Their success as railway contractors—The various professions followed by them—Their charity and hospitalities—Sir Jamsetjee's benefactions—Notices of the generous spirit of well-known Parsees.

WHEN it is remembered that the Parsees at Bombay, are the descendants of a small colony which emigrated from Persia in circumstances the most miserable, it is a matter of some surprise to strangers in India, that this people have simultaneously with the progress of British power in India risen into affluence and importance, while the other natives of the land, Mahomedans and Hindoos, have fallen into insignificance. The ancestors of the present race were remarkable for their warlike, enterprising, and industrious spirit.

If ever called to arms, the present Parsees will not be found wanting in the courage which distinguished their ancestors, but living under a Government which they consider quite paternal, and having no political interest in the land, there is nothing for them to fight for, and they have consequently concentrated all their strength in the two latter qualities of their ancient race, industry and enterprise.

These qualities in which the other natives of India are sadly deficient, have given to the Parsees that position which they now hold. On their arrival in India the Parsees chiefly employed themselves as cultivators of the soil, and as artisans. They followed these pursuits for about a thousand years, but no sooner did they perceive that there were openings for gaining wealth and distinction, than the spirit which had laid dormant for nearly ten centuries, burst forth again with renewed vigour and power.

To the British power in India the Parsees are chiefly indebted for their present position. Under its authority their commercial spirit revived, and they began for the first time to reap the fruit of their own industry. The native governments of India had invariably acted as a check to industry and enterprise—no man could enjoy the fruits of his own labour, as the people were constantly subjected to the caprice of the ruler, and the tyranny and oppression of his innumerable hosts of subordinate officers.

The cause of the depressed, ignoble, and cowardly spirit of the Hindoos, can safely be traced to the system pursued by those Governments under which they had groaned for thousands of years. The accession of British power in India was therefore a godsend to the Parsees; it enabled them to enter upon higher and nobler pursuits, and at once removed those restraints which the tyrannical rule of native princes had imposed upon them. Dadysett, Pestonjee and Hormusjee Wadia, the earliest Parsees of wealth and influence, had by their individual enterprise, raised themselves from obscurity to a distinguished position.

Almost all the Parsee Shets now living, have been the creators of their own fortunes. Sir Jamsetjee Jeejeebhoy, whose name is known in almost every part of the world, as the first merchant prince in India, was the son of poor parents. Shet Framjee Nusserwanjee, Shet Cowasjee Jehangir, Shet Manackjee Nusserwanjee, and a number of other Parsee gentlemen, reputed for their wealth, have also been the architects of their own fortunes. And how have all these attained their present position? By their commercial enterprise and remarkable industry. Wherever wealth is to be acquired, or wherever the English standards have been carried, the Parsees have followed with the fearless energy of men who required but the simple assurance that the protection of English law and English justice would be thrown around them. The Parsee tradesman followed the British army to Cabul, and is now to be found in every city of India, foremost in every enterprise, and ready to take advantage of every opening. We may be forgiven the boast, but we can safely say, that in the short space of a century, we have placed ourselves in competition with the merchant princes of the English Babylon, and no history of the commerce of the East would be complete without a prominent place being given to the mercantile houses established by the Parsees in India and China. Even London, the great commercial metropolis of the world, possesses a Parsee mercantile house. Those wealthy and spirited Camas, who can justly boast of possessing first-rate mercantile houses in

India and China, opened a similar house in London about three years ago, and Messrs. Cama and Co. are daily seen in Gresham House, carrying on extensive commercial intercourse. It is the first Parsee house established in London, and its projectors are consequently entitled to no little praise for their enterprising spirit.

No question has ever been raised as to the commercial morality of the Parsees; they are upright and honourable in their dealings. Between themselves written agreements are unknown; their word is truly "their bond," and this system they extend to most Europeans with whom they have dealings. Being incapable themselves of dishonesty in such matters, they willingly believe that others are actuated by similar honourable feelings.

In the establishment in India of banks and various other joint-stock companies, the Parsees have been the prime movers. They have shared largely in the introduction in India of railways, those great pioneers of civilization and commerce. They are extensive landholders, and the finest houses in the Island of Bombay are owned by them. A number of them are ship-owners. In short, much of the prosperity of Bombay is owing to the commercial spirit and activity of the Parsees. They have aided considerably, both by their influence and wealth, all projects for public improvements. There is not a single measure, having for its aim the good of the public, which has not received a handsome contribution from the purse of a Parsee.

One instance of remarkable industry and a love for the extension of agriculture in India, requires prominent notice. The late Framjee Cowasjee, Esq., who, for half a century, was one of the most enlightened, liberal-minded, energetic, upright, and honourable merchants, was the greatest native improver in the Bombay Presidency, for which manifestation of public spirit he was justly styled the Earl of Leicester of India. On his estate at Powai, about eighteen miles from Bombay, he introduced the cultivation of cotton and tea, and planted a great quantity of sugar canes, indigo, and mulberries for silkworms, and a large number of other valuable growths of the soil. Though he did not succeed to the extent of his desires, he converted the place from a forest into a fertile estate, yielding a net revenue of 20,000 rupees, or 2,000*l.* per annum.

Framjee Cowasjee was the first Parsee, we may safely say, the first and only native of India who, in the year 1838, sent a present of that sweet and delicious fruit the Bombay mangoes, to her Most Gracious Majesty the Queen.* The labours of this venerable old man will be best understood by a perusal of the following extract. Sir John Malcolm, in

* The following is the document which accompanied the ffering:—

"To Her Most Gracious Majesty the Queen of England.

"May it please your Majesty,

"The improvement and extension of steam navigation have now happily brought your Majesty's dominions at home and your dominions in the Eastern world so closely together, that I venture most humbly and most respectfully to lay at your Majesty's feet some specimens of the celebrated Bombay Mangoes, in the earnest hope that this delicious fruit, which has never before been transmitted to Europe, may reach your Majesty in a state of preservation and prove acceptable.

"Such precautions have been adopted to preserve the fruit as appear most efficacious, but if the botanists of your Majesty's dominions at home can prescribe a preferable method, it shall be adopted in the transmission of further supplies of this or any other kind of fruit peculiar to the country which has not hitherto been seen in Great Britain.

"Your Majesty's most dutiful and faithful
"Eastern subject,
"FRAMJEE COWASJEE.

"*Bombay*, 18*th May*, 1838."

In acknowledgment of this present, the Master of the Household conveyed to him the Queen's approbation of the zeal and enterprise evinced by him, and her Majesty's gratification at the dutiful expression of loyalty by which it was accompanied.

his administration of India, thus speaks of Powai under the head of improvements in Salsett:—

"A grant was given to Framjee of the fine estate of Powai, in perpetuity, at a moderate quit rent, on an understanding that certain improvements were to be made. My minute of the 30th of November, 1830, fully explains how far that good and able man has realized these expectations; I shall therefore quote it as the best illustration of the consequences that have already resulted from the measures adopted to promote the prosperity of Salsett. I lately paid a visit to the estate of Framjee Cowasjee at Powai, and never was more gratified. This highly respectable native has laid out much money in a variety of useful improvements; he has sunk a number of wells, has built houses, made an excellent road, planted a great quantity of sugar cane, indigo, and mulberries for silkworms; he has erected an excellent sugar mill, which I saw at work, and all the necessary buildings of an indigo manufactory. But what I was most delighted with was the passionate fondness Framjee appeared to have for his estate. His projected improvements of a tank, a garden full of fruit trees of every country, the erection of a bungalow for English travellers, and a serai and stables at the spot where the road to his estate leaves the Tannah great road, will be most useful to the public, as it is exactly half-way between Bombay and Tannah, and mark the liberal spirit in which he has determined to fulfil the obligation of his lease.

"'He evidently thinks less of profit than of being the first native improver of the soil on a scale that will match the science and enterprise of a European settler. His ambition is directed by the possession of this fine estate to the object of being a country gentleman; and whatever be the pecuniary result to him of his speculation, he will gain much in health, reputation, and enjoyment, while Government will eventually have a hundred-fold for any petty immediate or prospective sacrifices it may have made in the mere value of the land or its produce.

"I was so gratified by what Framjee showed me of his actual improvements, and the plans he had in contemplation, that I regretted not having provided myself with an appropriate token of my marked approbation of his public spirit, and of the benefits that might be derived from his example. To remedy this forgetfulness, I presented him, on the spot, with my own valuable watch and chain, expressing at the same time, before the gentlemen who accompanied me and a crowd of the natives employed or settled on his estate, my delight with what I had witnessed, and the gratification I should have in conveying to the Board and to my superiors in England information of all I had seen, and my sense of the value of such improvements as he had made and projected, both to the Government and to the country. Framjee Cowasjee was delighted with the approbation I gave him. He would persevere, he said, whatever discouragement he might at first meet with in his plans: my watch, he added, should be preserved in his family; and he deemed the gift bestowed on the spot, and in the manner it was, as rendering stronger than ever the pledge he had given to Government to improve in every way the lands they have granted him."

The same distinguished statesman bears testimony to the intelligence and enterprise of the Parsees in the following words:—"There is no body of natives in India so remarkable for their intelligence and enterprise as the Parsees. Bombay has owed its advancement in a great degree to this class; and in the actual condition of this presidency it appears to me a political consideration of much importance to strengthen their attachment to Government by new ties which are of a nature calculated to combine the promotion of their interests with those of the state. Salsett is recommended to them by its vicinity to Bombay, its excellent roads, and security. It may not yield the profit they anticipate, but they will render it a garden, and free us from trouble and expense in its management; and above all, it will give to the wealthy and public-spirited men that interest in the soil, and that knowledge of the benefits of works like roads, canals, and bridges, which may be of the greatest use, both as it disposes them to embark in works that advance the interests of Government and the general prosperity of this presidency. The feelings which will be inspired, and the knowledge attained by men of this class being landholders in Salsett, will gradually lead them to the Conkan and Deccan, where such persons are much required to promote plans of improvement, without which these countries will never pay the expenses of their occupation and management."

How eager a Parsee is to betake himself to any profession, will be best judged of from the fact that no sooner was railway enterprise introduced into India than several of the race found employment for themselves as contractors for the construction of railroads. In a field of labour entirely new to them, they have made a name and attained distinction. Jamsetjee Dorabjee is now considered the foremost native railway contractor in India. This Parsee began his railway career by tendering unsuccessfully for the first two contracts on the line from Bombay to Thanna. His offer for the third contract was accepted at a very considerable reduction of the estimate of the chief engineer, and the manner in which it was executed gave every satisfaction.

Jamsetjee next undertook to construct three large viaducts, each of them nearly 200 yards long, and over fifty feet in height. At this time it was predicted that the work was beyond his strength, or more than he could perform, but it was finished within the appointed time, and in the words of the chief engineer, Mr. Berkeley, "in a style worthy of any contractor, of any country, and of the approbation of any engineer." He again took another contract of twenty miles from Callian to Narel; and again a further length of seventeen miles from Narel to Campoolee, at the foot of the Bhore Ghaut, all of which he executed to the satisfaction of the railway authorities.

In the year 1857, Jamsetjee Dorabjee obtained, by public competition, from the directors of the Great Indian Peninsula Railway, in London, a contract for the construction of a further twenty-six miles of their line, extending from Wasind to Kustsarah, at the foot of the Thul Ghaut incline. These works are very formidable, and partake very much of the same character as the great works which are being executed on the two Ghaut inclines. They lie in a difficult and unfavourable district, nearly covered with jungle, full of trap hills and mountain torrents; unhealthy in places, difficult of access, devoid of water during the hot season, and thinly populated.

The contract is a large one, amounting probably to nearly 200,000*l.*, and the Parsee contractor has undertaken to complete the works by the month of December, 1859, in a period of little more than two years. It comprises about 1,000,000 cubic yards of embankment and many heavy rock cuttings. Also four large viaducts, of which one consists of six 50 feet arches 100 feet high, another of seven 30 feet arches 50 feet high, a third of seven 50 feet arches 100 feet high, and the fourth of three 50 feet arches 70 feet high. It also contains a large mass of masonry, in numerous smaller bridges and culverts, in addition to which, the contractor has undertaken to construct all the stations.

His arrangements for this great work have been workman-like and comprehensive. He has largely availed himself of native agency, and has entrusted the practical superintendence to several Europeans of acknowledged abilities and experience, who have received liberal appointments from him. He has employed, notwithstanding the great demand for labour, 17,000 hands, and by judicious provisions for their health and necessities, has succeeded in keeping the greater portion of them upon the works during the unfavourable part of the year. He has exhibited considerable judgment and foresight in the preparations which he has made, and which will enable him to cope successfully with the unusual difficulty of his contract.

The progress of his works has been rapid, and he has given entire satisfaction to the

Company, by his exertions and his care and liberality in the execution of the works which he has undertaken. When this contract is completed, Jamsetjee Dorabjee will have constructed ninety miles of railway, or the whole of the line upon the Concan, except the four miles between Tannah and Perseek, which were made by Messrs. Wythes and Jackson.

We here subjoin a table showing the professions and number of Parsees as given in the last census of Bombay, which cannot fail to be interesting. The number here given, denotes the females and minors, as included in the profession of the head of the family:

Annuitants, independents	2,657
Auctioneers	128
Bakers, confectioners	1,417
Bullock drivers	97
Cane workers	474
Clothiers, drapers, mercers	328
Cotton workers or retailers	124
Domestic servants	5,468
Fishmongers	13
Grain dealers	5
Hawkers	347
Horse dealers, drivers	2,025
Iron dealers	8
Jewellers and watchmakers	1,125
Labourers	41
Liquor sellers, distillers, palm wine drawers	5,227
Marine store dealers	37
Medical men	577

Merchants, bankers, or brokers . . .	61,298
Money changers, assayers	1,535
Oil dealers	163
Pensioners	1,274
Policeman	1
Priests	5,656
Printers, stationers, bookbinders . . .	616
Schoolmasters	2,056
Tailors, embroiderers, tent makers . .	172
Tavernkeepers	826
Vagrants	127
Water carriers	1,584
Wood workers and dealers	4,101
Writers and accountants	11,028
Total .	110,544

It will be seen from this table, that the largest number, or more than one-half of the whole Parsee population, follow the avocations of merchants, bankers, or brokers, which fact furnishes a clear proof of the commercial bent of the Parsee mind. It will also be seen from the table that the commoner trades, such as butchers, barbers, laundrymen, palkee-bearers, sweepers, or scavengers, are not resorted to by them.

It may, perhaps, strike the reader as curious that the Parsees, whose ancestors were remarkable for their martial spirit, have not embraced the profession of arms. The matter can be easily explained. We must, in the first place, observe that there is no objection whatever to a Parsee embracing the profession of a soldier on religious grounds, as is erroneously supposed by Europeans. The veneration the Parsees have for fire has been the groundwork of this supposition, and on this belief it is surmised that they would not fire a gun or pistol. This idea, however, is simply ridiculous. The Parsees hold fire in veneration in the sense which will be explained in the chapter on religion, but this circumstance offers no impediment to their employing fire-arms as offensive or defensive weapons. When the Parsees were lately apprehensive of a disturbance in Bombay, the shops in the place were cleared of guns and pistols by the Parsees.

We must look for the real reason of the Parsees not becoming soldiers, in the fact that very little or no inducement is offered to them to enlist in the army. The native (Hindoo or Mahomedan) soldiers are paid seven rupees, or fourteen shillings a month, inclusive of rations, while a Parsee, in the lowest employment that he can enter upon, namely, that of a cook or domestic servant, earns nearly double the sum which is paid to the sepoy. During the late mutinies, when Bombay was denuded of

European troops, many Parsees were willing to enlist in the army if the pay of European soldiers was accorded to them. We have not the slightest hesitation in saying that the Parsees would be found to be as good and brave soldiers as the Anglo-Saxons, whilst their loyalty and attachment to the Government they would be called upon to serve, would always be above suspicion.

In the foregoing list, the number of writers and accountants stands at 11,028. Of these, nearly half are in the service of Government, which, when we consider the total number of natives in Government employ, shows only a small percentage of Parsee officials. Indeed, the Parsees have not found extensive employment in the public service. The native functionaries, and other servants of Government, are chiefly drawn from among the Hindoos and Mahomedans. But it is a matter of no little gratification to us to mention, that whenever any one of this tribe has been placed by Government in some responsible post, requiring considerable ability, energy, and judgment, he has been found fully equal to the task. At the present day, one Parsee is a Judge of the Court of Small Causes at Bombay, another is the

Translator and Interpreter in her Majesty's Supreme Court, one a Deputy-Magistrate in one of the zillas of the Bombay presidency, three or four are Assistant-Commissioners in the Nagpore territories, and about half a dozen are Sudur Ameens, or native judges.

All these gentlemen, it is well known, perform the responsible duties of their offices ably and satisfactorily.

A very few Parsees have served Government in political employment.* The services

* A number of Parsees are members of a political body called the Bombay Association, formed for the purpose of obtaining reforms in the government of the country. Though the president of this association, the much respected Jagonuthjee Sunkersett, Esq., and his son, Venoyeklon Jagonuthjee, Esq., one of the secretaries, are Hindoos, most of the chief members are Parsees. The position taken up by this body is not one of antagonism to Government, nor is the constant decrying of all its measures the aim of the association. Its object is rather to obtain information from unprejudiced sources, which to the authorities might be sealed up, and to lay it before the Government and suggest remedial measures. Every one of its members is fully sensible of the benefits they enjoy under British rule. We cannot do better than quote the sentiments on the subject of the senior secretary, Mr. Nowasjee Furdoonjee, delivered at a public meeting, from which the feelings of the members of the association towards the Government will be best judged.

"Let us for a while examine the character and policy of the British Government, under whose sway we have the good fortune to be placed. This liberal and enlightened Government has conceded several important and valuable privileges, of a Parsee named Khurshedjee Modee, with the political embassy at Poona, at the Court of the Peshwa, are well described by Grant Duff, in his history of the Maharattas. The late Ardasír Dhunjeeshaw, Bahadoor of Surat, and his ancestors, have done immense service to the Government. Mr. H. G. Briggs, a name not unfamiliar in literary circles in Bombay, in his work entitled

and has conferred on us several boons for which we ought to be thankful. I will here enumerate a few of them which affect and exercise a powerful influence on our social progress. The first is civil and political liberty, which consists in the power of thinking and acting with perfect independence, just as we deem fit, without any restraint or control on the part of our rulers, except from the laws of nature, which wisely and properly impose certain restrictions that are necessary for our safety and welfare. The second is religious liberty or toleration, which is the free right of adopting and maintaining opinions on religious subjects, and of worshipping the Almighty according to the dictates of our conscience, and the doctrines of our respective religions, without any interference or control on the part of Government or any private individual. It cannot be denied that these privileges were either withheld *in toto*, or greatly abridged and unjustly curtailed under the former dynasty of rulers. The prosperity and greatness of the British nation depend mainly on the possession and enjoyment of these privileges, which are the birthrights of every British subject: and the British Government, in consonance to the enlightened and liberal policy which they have thought proper to adopt towards the people of this country, having conceded to the latter the full enjoyment of these rights, the chief cause which operated as a check to native improvement and progress has thereby been removed."

"Cities of Gujarashtra," gives a brief but accurate summary of Ardeshir's distinguished services. So well has Mr. Briggs treated the subject, that we shall be excused for quoting his remarks. He says:—

"Among the natives of Western India he (Ardasír) stands alone for his abilities, his energy, and his unwearied zeal for the Government he served, the country which gave him birth and his countrymen refuge in exile. To form any idea of the state of Surat at this time, and to appreciate the exertions of Ardasír, it must be borne in mind that both the city and the river were plagued with robbers and pirates equally daring and adroit. The indolent avariciousness of the citizen was exposed to the rapacity of his needy neighbour, at whose means the villanous Koli of Gujarat could be introduced into his dwelling; and the nature of such felonies was frequently rendered more atrocious by the commission of murder: but the stealthiness and security with which such feats were performed wholly defeated the aim and the ends of justice.

"Nor was the system of piracy any half-handed measure: the *Gifts of the Ocean* (the happy sobriquet) were shared from Cambay north, as far southward as Daman—by a leagued fraternity, whose emissaries were too frequently the servants or friends of the enterprising merchant. It was nothing unusual to learn of singular storms and stranger shipwrecks; yet Swali Nest or Thari Hole had received many hundred bales of cotton or richer spoil both unsoiled by the sea and unknown to any voyage but that of the river. The gains were equally distributed; which permitted the existence of the band such a series of years. But, even this nefarious, audacious, and extensive plot, perished under proper vigilance and due discrimination.

"Mr. Anderson, lately Governor of Bombay, a man of severe thought and determined principles of action—when session judge of Surat, had bestowed some attention on this subject, but was at fault as to the means of extirpating these evils, and he bent his eye upon a young and adventurous instrument for accomplishing the required purpose: his penetration of character found in Ardasír the willing engine. From this period is to be dated the extraordinary exertions of Ardasír for Surat; instantly diverting his notice to the amount and nature of the existing sore, he probed their extent, and then resorted to remedial steps.

"The employment of his energies for the state did not terminate in the suppression of the grievances noticed: they were followed, by remodelling the police of the city—the introduction of an establishment of doudias, or watchmen—an improved gaol discipline, quite as well as the foundation of a paper manufactory to engage the time of the prisoners in salutary pursuits, and the improvement of the roads. Amid these trying labours he devoted a large portion of his time in rendering considerable assistance to Mr. Borrodaile, of the civil service, in a valuable work prepared for the Government, which that gentleman had the candour to admit without Ardasír's services the undertaking must have failed.

"The intricate, the substantial, the important services of Ardasír induced the Government in November, 1825, to bestow upon him a khilat, or honorary garb, in that manner most gratifying to the pride of the recipient. The ceremony was performed in open durbar by the agent for the honourable the Governor, and the opportunity availed of to present Ardasír with 5,000 rupees. On this occasion a petition, signed by 800 of the principal native residents of Surat, was delivered to the agent, expressive of the pleasure experienced in this prominent notice of the efforts of their fellow-citizen for the general security and weal of the community.

"Upon the 22nd of December, 1829, and during his stay at Surat, Sir John Malcolm, the then Governor of Bombay, by way of particularly marking the meritorious labours of Ardasír, at a special durbar held, to which were summoned all the principal personages in and about Surat, invested him with a khilat, and conferred the title of bahadur—in themselves no ordinary honours, but which in this instance were accompanied by the presentation of a horse with rich trappings, and a jaghir of the annual rental of 3,000 rupees, promising Ardasír, at the same time, to send him a gold medal. Upwards of 20,000 natives had assembled to witness the ceremony, and to signify their thanks to the Governor for the honours paid Ardasír. General Hessman was ordered to afford a strong military force to give importance to the occasion, and a company of infantry escorted Ardasír, with a military band, to his residence.

"In 1830, the Judicial Commissioner, Mr. James Sutherland, having received special instructions from the Government of Bombay, held a durbar on the 14th of December to carry into effect the intentions of the honourable the Governor in presenting Ardasír with the promised medal. In the presence of a large concourse, composed of European and native gentlemen, after a long, eloquent, and appropriate speech in Hindoostani, detailing the several valuable and useful services rendered by Ardasír to the state and the community of Surat, and ably expatiating upon the high sense entertained by Government of this public servant, Mr. Sutherland delivered to Ardasír the gift of the Bombay Cabinet. It is a plain round slab of gold, bearing the following inscription on one side, "This medal is presented to Ardasír Dunjeeshah Bahadoor, Kotwal of Surat, in token of the high sense entertained by the Bombay Government of the diligence and fidelity with which he has performed his public duties both as an officer of police and in other capacities. 1st January, 1830." The obverse bears a translation in Gujarati.

"Years have since fled, and Ardasír's unremitting ability, his unwearied zeal—remain unaltered; his assistance in the general affairs of the country, have continued to prove the theme of all his superiors. His counsel has been frequently sought, his opinion never disregarded; and his merits were found of no ordinary calibre in the diplomatic arrangements required in the affairs of native states, particularly those of the Nawabs of Surat and Suchin and the Rana of Dharampur. In the last matter where the pecuniary embarrassments of the prince had been so promptly and satisfactorily arranged while Ardasír was native agent to the Governor, the Hindoo chieftain, in grateful recollection of the Zoroastrian's intervention, summarily thrust upon him a village affording a yearly revenue of two thousand rupees, which Ardasír, with his usual spirit, declined to accept; a reference was subsequently submitted by the Rana to the Bombay Government on the subject, and the expected negative reply ensued."

The European reader will thus see, that of all the races inhabiting India, the Parsees are the most intelligent and energetic. Not trammelled by that cursed system of "Caste," they are at liberty to trade and inhabit all quarters of the globe, and follow whatever professions they think will be conducive to their advancement in life. They may justly boast that, upon the first opportunity the race has possessed for a thousand years of rising into eminence, they have proved themselves the worthy descendants of a renowned ancestry.

Although insignificant in point of numbers, the Parsee community can never be absent from the European mind, when contemplating the vast empire of India. The Parsee has been flatteringly described as the Saxon of the East, and under the ægis of the just and enlightened rule of England has entered, with success, into competition with the Saxon of the West in the meed for honourable distinction.*

The wealth acquired by the Parsees, we are proud to say, is rarely mis-spent. There are, of course, as in all communities, some who wisely hoard up their riches, while others squander away large fortunes in luxury and debauchery without contributing a penny towards any charitable fund or object of public utility. But it cannot be denied that the majority of the Parsees are benevolent to a degree; some even forget that charity begins at home, and are liberal beyond their means. The race has inherited this spirit of liberality from its ancestors, who were con-

* Rustomjee Byramjee, a graduate of the Grant Medical College, obtained in 1857, by public competition, a commission as Assistant Surgeon on the Bombay establishment.

spicuous for their love of charity. It is enough to show to a Parsee an object deserving of relief or support, and his purse is at once opened.

This good quality which flows in the Parsee veins has been noticed by the earliest Europeans, who came in contact with this people. The benevolence of one Sorabjee Muncherjee is thus referred to in a Bombay newspaper, dated 1790. "We are happy in the opportunity of pointing out the liberality of Sorabjee Muncherjee, whose conduct does honour to humanity. During the present scarcity of provisions, he daily feeds upwards of 2,000 people, of different castes, at his own expense."

Mrs. Graham, in her journal of a residence in India in the years 1805 and 1806, says, "the Parsee merchant, Ardeshir Dady, fed five thousand people, besides contributing in other ways towards the support of the starving population." The Rev. Mr. Ovington, who has published an account of his voyage to Surat in the year 1689, has said that "the Parsees are ever ready to provide for the sustenance and comfort of such as want them. Their universal kindness, either in employing such as are needy and able to work, or bestowing a seasonable bounteous charity to such as are infirm and miserable, leave no man destitute of relief, nor suffer a beggar in all their tribe, and herein so far comply with that excellent rule of Pythagoras, to enjoy a kind of community among friends." Major Moore, in his narrative of the operation of Captain Little's detachment, &c., says, "The benevolence of the Parsees is not restricted to persons of their own sect. Their industry and extensive mercantile spirit have enabled many of them to amass considerable fortunes, which they spend with generous profusion in acts of charity and hospitality."

But let us come nearer to our own times. Who has not heard of that very prince of munificence, the venerable Parsee baronet, Sir Jamsetjee Jeejeebhoy, whose unbounded charity is not only unsurpassed, but without a parallel in ancient or modern times. Since 1822, when his charitable acts began to be publicly noticed, scarcely a year has passed in which he has not displayed that spirit of liberality which has made his name so famous throughout the world, and brought upon him the blessings and regard of his people and unprecedented honours from his gracious Sovereign.

The capital of Western India, and Surat, Nowsari, and other places in Guzerat, and Khandalla and Poona in the Deccan, bear testimony to his liberality, philanthropy, and public spirit. He has at various times released the prisoners confined in jail for debt under the authority of the Small Cause Court; built causeways for the benefit of the public and the promotion of traffic between Bombay and Salsett; founded schools and colleges for the education of his countrymen; erected hospitals for the relief of the suffering poor; established benevolent institutions for relieving the indigent and poor at Bombay, Surat, Nowsaree, and other places; built spacious and comfortable dharumsallas for the convenience of travellers; and erected works for the supply of water, and relieved people from the scarcity of the most precious of all commodities.

Sir Jamsetjee's subscriptions to various charitable objects have always been handsome and extensive, while we cannot guess the extent of his private charity. To the poor, the needy, and the distressed, he has always held out a helping hand. Nor are his charities confined to people of his own caste or race; he gives indiscriminately without reference to caste, colour, or creed. So widely had the fame of his munificence spread, that in 1842 he received the honour of knighthood from the hands of our gracious and most beloved Sovereign, Queen Victoria. The patent of knighthood * was, amidst great ostentation and public demonstration, presented to Sir Jamsetjee, at the Government-house at Parel, by Sir George Anderson, then Governor of Bombay. On the 15th of December, 1843, Sir Jamsetjee received a further mark of her Majesty's approbation of his generosity and public spirit

* The following account of the armorial bearings of Sir Jamsetjee Jeejeebhoy is taken from a newspaper of the day:—

"Sir Jamsetjee Jeejeebhoy's 'coat of arms' consists of a handsome shield in the form of the shields used by the Knights of St. John at the defence of Malta, beautifully emblazoned by scrolas of gold. At the lower part of the shield is a landscape scene in India, intended to represent a part of the island of Bombay, with the islands of Salsette and Elephanta in the distance. The sun is seen rising from behind Salsette to denote industry, and in diffusing its light and heat displaying liberality. The upper part of the shield has a white ground to denote integrity and purity, on which are placed two bees representing industry and perseverance. The shield is surmounted by a crest consisting of a beautiful peacock, denoting wealth, grandeur, and magnificence; and in its mouth is placed an ear of paddy, denoting beneficence. Below the shield is a white pennant folded, on which is inscribed the words 'Industry and Liberality,' which is Sir Jamsetjee's motto."

in the shape of a gold medal * set in diamonds.

His grateful countrymen were not, however, behind hand in recognising and publicly testifying their respect for the good qualities which distinguish this great man. In the month of June, 1856, a public meeting, organised by the native population of Bombay, and cordially supported by the Europeans of the city, was held in the Town Hall of Bombay, under the presidency of the Right Hon. the Governor, Lord Elphinstone. The object of the demonstration was to vote a statue to the venerable Sir Jamsetjee Jeejeebhoy, to be set up in the Town Hall, where the effigy of the first native of India will be placed, by the side of those of Elphinstone, Malcolm, and Forbes.

Excellent speeches were delivered at the meeting, two of which we are tempted to reprint, as they not only fully describe the excellent qualities of Sir Jamsetjee, but as they are the spontaneous expressions of two men high in authority in India, they will carry greater conviction with them than the

* The medal bears, on its face, the image of the Queen encircled with diamonds. The reverse bears this inscription: "Sir Jamsetjee Jeejeebhoy, Bart., from the British Government, in honour of his munificence and his patriotism."

opinions which emanate from one who belongs to Sir Jamsetjee's own country and race.

The eloquent and impressive speech of Lord Elphinstone runs thus :—"When I was asked to preside over this meeting, I felt no ordinary satisfaction in accepting the invitation. The occasion was unusual, I believe I may say, in India, unprecedented. Every one must approve of the object so far, that every one must wish to do honour to Sir Jamsetjee Jeejeebhoy. Those who take an interest in the improvement and progress of the natives of this country must, I think, view our proceedings to-day with peculiar pleasure. It is a good sign when a community comes forward of its own accord to do homage to real worth; in honouring Sir Jamsetjee Jeejeebhoy, the community honours itself. The mere fact of this meeting renders it superfluous that I should expatiate upon Sir Jamsetjee Jeejeebhoy's claims to our respect and love. But I would point out that these do not rest solely upon the vast sums which he has contributed to objects of public charity and convenience. The extent, indeed, of those contributions is almost incredible; to enumerate the various benefits which he has conferred not only upon this town, but upon the presidency at large, would be to trespass unduly upon your time. I may, however, be permitted to observe that his public benefactions alone amount to a quarter of a million sterling—or exactly the sum which it will take to construct the great works which will supply this island with water. In what age, and in what country, can we find another example of such princely munificence? Three of the largest cities in Great Britain, Glasgow, Liverpool, and Manchester—whose united population, however, is not double that of Bombay—have lately incurred, or are at this moment incurring an expense of upwards of two millions sterling upon water-works. I will suppose that the united wealth of these three cities exceeds that of Bombay in the proportion that the cost of their water-works bears to ours. I must admit that this is no criterion at all, and that it is very probable that I have much under rated their superiority of wealth—but which of these cities, I ask, can boast of a citizen who has devoted 250,000*l.* to purposes of public charity and benevolence?

"But I have just said it is not the amount only of Sir Jamsetjee Jeejeebhoy's charities that commands my admiration. True liberality is shown in the manner of distribution no less than in the amount. I will not go back to the dark ages, and cite the times when Christian monasteries and Buddhist wickaras were endowed by men, who sought to gain the favour of Heaven by renouncing their possessions and performing what they considered an act of charity, and which was certainly one of abnegation. I may, however, refer to those who founded our great collegiate institutions, and to the monarchs who built the Hotel des Invalides at Paris, and Greenwich and Chelsea Hospitals near London. The former afforded education only to those who participated in the founder's faith. The latter were for the worn out soldiers and sailors of the kings who established them. Far be it from me to undervalue these noble foundations—but I cannot help remarking that Sir Jamsetjee's benefactions, with the sole exception I believe of the Parsee benevolent institution, are made to the entire community, not for Parsees only, but for Hindoos, Jews, Christians, and Mahomedans.

"It is this Catholic character of Sir Jamsetjee's benevolence—his sympathy for the poor and suffering of all castes and creeds—that has won for him the universal respect and esteem of all classes of the community, and it is to this feeling that we owe the gathering which the sheriff's requisition has collected to-day in this hall. The manner in which Sir Jamsetjee Jeejeebhoy acquired his great wealth was hardly less honourable to himself and beneficial to the community than the mode in which he dispenses it. By strict integrity, by industry and punctuality in all his commercial transactions, he has contributed to raise the character of the Bombay merchant in the most distant markets. His whole life is a practical illustration of the truth of the homely proverb—that "honesty is the best policy," and in this respect and in others he will leave behind him an example which I trust will long continue to be held up for imitation among us. But I have said enough, though certainly very far less than I might have said, upon Sir Jamsetjee Jeejeebhoy's claims upon our admiration and gratitude.

"I must not sit down without offering a few remarks upon the mode in which it is proposed that we should testify these sentiments. I hear that some object to a statue: it would be more consistent, they say, with the character of the man whom we seek to honour to make our tribute assume the shape of a work of charity than a work of art. I am unable to concur in this view. In the first place, I would remark that Sir Jamsetjee has anticipated us in every work of charity with which we might seek to connect his name. We have already hospitals, dhurumsallas, educational institutions, tanks, causeways, and I know not how many other things, intended for the relief and instruction and convenience of the people, called after him. Besides I think we may well wish to perpetuate among the worthies who have a place in this hall, or our public streets, the likeness of a man who has conferred such great benefits upon the community, and who will leave behind him so bright an example of all the qualities which dignify the acquisition of wealth, and render its possession a blessing.

"Most civilized nations, both in ancient and modern times, have adopted this mode of honouring distinguished public virtues and services. At Athens, we read that the porticos were crowded with statues, and at Rome the number in the forum became so great that the censor, P. Cornelius Scipio and M. Papilius, removed all those which had not been erected with the sanction of the senate and the people. It is not likely that such an accumulation will take place anywhere in modern times—least of all is it likely in India; but if it were possible, I would venture to predict that no future censor would be found to direct the removal of the statue of Sir Jamsetjee Jeejeebhoy from the spot where it is to be placed, and that it will remain to distant generations a monument of the civic virtues of the man, and of the gratitude of the community."

In an equally eloquent speech, H. L. Anderson, Esq., Secretary to Government, thus testified to the good qualities of Sir Jamsetjee:—"I feel that some apology is due from me for presenting myself to the meeting at so early a period of our proceedings. I may be permitted thus briefly to explain that, in undertaking to move this resolution, I have yielded to the opinion expressed to me, by several native gentlemen, that my near relationship to one of his oldest friends would render my performance of this duty acceptable to Sir Jamsetjee Jeejeebhoy. It has been also indirectly intimated to me that a similar feeling was entertained by Sir Jamsetjee's sons. Under these circumstances, and having very much at heart the object for which this meeting was convened, I have felt that I ought not to shrink from the work which has been thus assigned to me. In this hall we have frequently met to render our tribute of admiration to the heroes and statesmen who have illustrated the policy and the arms of our common country. This day we acquit ourselves of a duty dear to us all, of expressing our gratitude to one who, having acquired vast wealth by a long career of honourable industry, has distributed that wealth with unparalleled benevolence. The days are past when good deeds done in India remain unknown; this country is daily occupying a larger space in the minds of thoughtful men, and there is not a region on the civilized globe, from China to the far Republic of the West, which has not heard of the benevolent Knight of India. This island owes much to the public spirit of our native fellow citizens, it has enabled Bombay to maintain no unequal contest in the honourable emulation which progress must ever call forth between the three presidencies. I believe that gentlemen who have devoted their best energies to the interests of Calcutta and Madras have said, 'What could we not do if our natives were like the natives of Bombay.'

"Pre-eminent among those who have thus contributed to the prosperity of this presidency, is Sir Jamsetjee Jeejeebhoy. I fear that I should exhaust the patience of the meeting if I were to recount all the great public works which have been constructed by his munificence. I shall therefore only rapidly glance at some of the most prominent; but it ought not to be forgotten that, in addition to the great works which will endear his name to remote generations, his private—his almost secret—charities have divided the weekly bread to thousands of his fellow-creatures. The characteristic of his munificence has been enlightened usefulness.

"His wealth has been achieved by sagacity, industry, and the purest good faith; it has not been lavished with mere ostentatious and ill-considered profusion. In the long list of his public benefactions, there is not one which does not exhibit a wise discrimination, and amply deserve the title of a good work. Some have naturally been devoted to the relief and the improvement of the members of that ancient faith in which he was himself born and nurtured, but the greater portion have solely contemplated the common good of all. If a stranger landing on these shores were to inquire what were the works by which the Parsee Knight, of whom he had heard so much, had acquired his renown, we should but have to tell him 'to look around.' He would see hospitals which, besides the tender offices they have extended to the afflicted, have, in conjunction with the Grant College, conferred on India the inestimable benefit of a skilled body of native medical practitioners. He would see tanks, by which, to adopt the expression of Edmund Burke, the industry of man carefully husbands the precious gift of God. He would see, and not only here, but also at Nowsary in the north, and Khandallah in the south, dhurumsallas—the homes of charity, in which the houseless and the wandering find refuge and relief. He would see the noble causeway which unites the Islands of Bombay and Salsette. He would see the water-works at Poona, the bridges at Earla Parla and Bartha. He would see roads, wells, aqueducts, and reservoirs."

"But these works, great as they are, are very far from representing all the good deeds of Sir Jamsetjee Jeejeebhoy. He has founded and endowed an institution for the education and maintenance of the children of poor Parsees, at an expense of nearly 50,000*l*. Many of those whom I now address must have been present, as I was, when he gave in one gift to the sacred cause of education the sum of 30,000*l.*; and they will not easily forget the sensation created by that announcement made with so much calmness and simplicity. But besides founding the schools which bear his name, and besides contributing most liberally to various other educational institutions, he has proposed to give a new impetus to the native mind, to develope, if possible, another vein of talent by the formation of a school of design. To this great purpose he has devoted a sum of 10,000*l.* But it would be to gild refined gold to dwell on the abundant evidences of the public spirit of this excellent citizen.

"It will be sufficient for me to repeat what has been said by the noble lord in the chair, that he has expended, for the solid and enduring benefit of Bombay, no less a sum than a quarter of a million sterling. But in addressing a meeting at which many of my own countrymen are present, I must not fail to allude to the facts that, when the bones of thousands of heroic men—Europeans and sepoys—were whitening in the snows of Cabool, when famine decimated the Highlands of Scotland, when a mysterious dispensation of Providence deprived our poor Irishmen of their daily food, when the widows and the orphans of the brave men who died for the right at Alma and Inkermann, stretched forth their hands for aid, none evinced a more generous sympathy, none showed more alacrity in giving bread to the hungry, and binding up the wounds of the broken-hearted, than he whom this day we honour ourselves in honouring. If, gentlemen, such deeds as these go without recognition in his own generation, the shame will be ours. The bloodless triumphs of commerce have been illustrated by the ennobled names of Ashburton and Overstone. In the glorious temple which adorns the capital of the British Empire, in which lie the bones of the iron victor of a hundred fields, and the mutilated form of him,—

> 'The saviour of the silver coasted isle,
> The shaker of the Baltic and the Nile;'

—in that temple near the marble which gives to posterity the form of Samuel Johnson, stands the statue of the illustrious philanthropist, John Howard. Nor could learning and valour demand a worthier associate. Let us then, in the same spirit, give a great example to all India; let us show how a good man can be appreciated; and in this island, in which due reverence has been rendered to the genius of Wellesley and Elphinstone, to the virtues of Cornwallis and the gallant spirit of Malcolm, let us enable the humblest of his countrymen, in distant times, to gaze on the lineaments of their great benefactor. Such tributes are usually reserved for the illustrious dead. But in so mixed a population as that of Bombay, it is very meet that our venerable friend should know that all creeds and races, Parsees, Hindoos, Mussulmans, Jews, and Christians, have accorded to him their gratitude. That he should be assured by the concurrent voices of all, he has not laboured in vain, that he should see his good deeds, in the language of our great poet—

"'Formed in the applause
Where they are intended, and which like an arch reverberates
The voice again, or like a gate of steel,
Fronting the sun, receives and renders back
His figure and his heat.'

"He is now full of years. The evening of his days is brilliant with the lustre which anticipates the praises of posterity. Long may he husband out life's taper at the close, happy in his most estimable family—happy in the applause and affection of his fellow-citizens—happiest in the memory of his honourable and useful life."

Her Majesty has lately, we are glad to say, further honoured Sir Jamsetjee by conferring a baronetcy upon him. Mr. Cursetjee Jamsetjee, who is already so extensively known in society, is the heir-apparent to the baronetcy

We cannot conclude our short notice of this great man without appending a list of his benefactions so far as we have been able to ascertain them:

	Rupees
Sum paid for the relief of poor debtors in 1822, 1826, and 1842	3,040
Endowment for the performance in Bombay and Guzerat, of various Parsee rites and ceremonies .	1,80,000
Cost of a building and adjoining ground for the celebration of Public Festivals among the Parsees .	70,000
Contribution in money, grain, and clothes for the benefit of the sufferers by the great fire at Surat and Syed Poora	30,800
Sums remitted for the relief of poor Parsees at and near Surat, from 1840 to 1847	39,000
Subscriptions to the Panjrapol in Bombay . .	71,600
" " at Patton . .	3,000
Endowment for the relief of poor Hindoos in Guzerat, in memory of a Hindoo friend	30,000
Parsee cemeteries in various places	29,600
Sums given in aid of distressed members of native families	44,000
Building and repairs of various Parsee places of worship	16,700
Cost of sundry wells and reservoirs in Bombay and other places in the Presidency	15,000
Fund for the benefit of the poor blind at Nowsaree .	5,000
Subscriptions to the Parsee punchayet for charitable works	15,000

	Rupees
Parsee church at Poona	45,000
Dharumsalla at Khandalla	20,000
„ at Nowsaree	20,000
Fund for the funeral expenses of poor Parsees at Gundevee near Nowsaree	5,000
Redemption of the body-tax levied by the Gaikwad Government on the Parsees at Nowsaree	17,000
Endowment for poor Parsees at Nowsaree	62,500
„ „ „ at Surat	1,25,000
Buildings at Nowsaree for Parsee religious observances	8,400
Buildings connected with the cemetry at the same place	8,600
Contribution towards the construction of the J. J. hospital	1,60,500
The Obstetric Institution in connection with the J. J. hospital	30,000
Mahim causeway	1,55,000
Mahim road	22,000
Bridge at Arla Parla	4,000
Tank at Bandora	6,500
Dharumsalla, Bellasis road, Bombay	1,50,000
Water-works at Poona	1,80,270
Bridge at Bartha near Surat	7,300
Tank on the Byculla road	23,000
Endowment to the Parsee Benevolent Institution for the education and maintenance of the children of poor Parsees at Bombay	4,40,000
School of design in Bombay	1,00,000
A Zend Avasta school for Parsees	3,000
Book and prize fund Grant Medical College	15,000
Subscription to the Parsee punchayet for charitable works	15,000
Contribution to the fund for the benefit of European pensioners and their widows	5,000
Subscription to the Elphinstone Professorships	11,500
„ Byculla schools	1,000

	Rupees
Subscription to District Benevolent Society, Bombay	5,006
„ Sailors Home, Bombay	2,000
„ Shivry School of Industry (founded by Dr. Buist)	1,500
„ Free school, Calcutta	2,000
„ Fund for the relief of the Scotch and Irish .	10,000
„ Naval school at Devonport	1,000
„ Wellington Testimonial	7,000
„ Patriotic Fund	5,000
„ Relief Fund	2,000
„ Havelock Testimonial	1,000
Total Rupees	2,219,810
Total Sterling	£221,981

It would be a great injustice were we to altogether fail in noticing the charitable and generous spirit of other Parsee gentlemen. Framjee Nusserwanjee, Esq., is well known both to the native and European community of Bombay for his great liberality; there is scarcely any charitable object which does not receive some assistance from his purse. He was one of the four Parsee gentlemen who mainly contributed towards the establishment of the Parsee Girls' Schools, and he is at this day one of its warmest supporters. He has of late evinced such an interest in the education and general enlightenment of his countrymen that any measure tending to further this object receives his best sympathies, and his purse is ever ready to minister to the wants of institutions which have for their object the promotion of the welfare and advancement of the people.

Cowasjee Jehanjeer, Esq., has also by his generous acts established a claim upon the gratitude of the poor. Without noticing his handsome subscriptions to various charities, one or two of his acts deserve prominent mention. Two years ago he contributed a sum of 30,000 rupees to the fund for relieving indigent Parsees; and with the view of encouraging young men of his race to prosecute their studies for a lengthened period, he has founded a scholarship in the Sir Jamsetjee Jeejeebhoy Parsee Benevolent Institution, towards the support of which he has likewise given a handsome sum.

Manockjee Nusserwanjee, Esq., an equally generous man, beloved by the poor and honoured by his people, on the death of his wife* set apart 30,000 rupees for different charitable institutions; and his contributions to charitable purposes are invariably characterised by great liberality. On the death of

* The Parsees, on the death of a near relative, generally contribute to a charitable fund.

the late Jeejeebhoy Dadabhoy, Esq., a fund of 2,00,000 rupees was set apart in his will; the interest of the sum was from time to time to be contributed to such objects of charity as the trustees thought proper. Byramjee Jeejeebhoy, Esq., the son of the deceased, is an equally liberal man.

The wealthy individuals who compose the Cama family are all ever ready to meet the calls of humanity. On the death of the late Nusserwanjee Muncherjee Cama, his sons voluntarily set aside a fund of 1,25,000 rupees for different charitable institutions. This spirit of liberality is highly commendable, as it displays on the part of the sons of the deceased a generous self-denial in applying a handsome sum of money to noble purposes which otherwise would have been their own.

We could thus go on enumerating instance after instance to prove the benevolent and generous nature of this race. It is possible that the foregoing notices may wound the feelings of those whose names we have mentioned, but in a work like the present it would be impossible to leave such noble acts unrecorded. It is solely owing to the benevolence of the wealthy Parsees that not a single Parsee beggar is to be seen, a fact highly creditable to the race. The committee of the Bombay District Benevolent Society* thus publicly acknowledged the fact in one of their reports, "The public at large owe a debt of gratitude to the Parsees of Bombay, for not one beggar of that caste has ever applied to this society for relief, nor is a Parsee pauper ever to be seen in our streets."

* This institution is supported by Government, its officers, and the European and native gentlemen.

CHAPTER VI.

EDUCATION.

Education of males—Female education—Future prospects upon the increasing desire for learning—Notices of rich men's sons devoting themselves to study.

We now proceed to the consideration of the progress of education among the Parsees. Of all the natives of India this race has shown itself the most desirous of receiving the benefits of an English education; and their eagerness to drink the waters of the science and literature of the West has been conspicuous.

The commencement of the educational movement with the Parsees can only be dated as far back as twenty-five or thirty years ago. Before the establishment, in the year 1820, of the Bombay Native Education Society by the Hon. Mountstuart Elphinstone, the great benefactor of the people of India, only a few schools existed at Bombay for imparting instruction in English. These seminaries were conducted by half-educated Indo-Britons, and the scholars were chiefly Parsees. The accession of the above-mentioned enlightened statesman to the Governorship of Bombay was the commencement of an educational era in that presidency; as the Governors who preceded him had made no attempts to instruct their subjects. The Hon. Mountstuart Elphinstone, therefore, is fully entitled to the honour of being called the first European in the Bombay Presidency who evidenced a deep interest in the education and welfare of the natives. In the year 1820 he established the Bombay Native Education Society, for the education of native youth. The Parsees were the first to benefit by the opening of this school; thus clearly showing, at the very earliest opportunity which presented itself, their eagerness and desire for education. As this infant tree grew in strength, the valuable fruit it yielded was recognised as a great boon by the people, and its extension was extremely desired by the natives themselves.

An opportunity for the fulfilment of their wishes soon presented itself. On the Hon. Mountstuart Elphinstone's retirement from the Governorship of Bombay, the natives of the island, among whom the Parsees took a prominent part, subscribed among themselves large sums of money, and raised a fund for the establishment and maintenance of a college for the education of their countrymen in the higher branches of European science and literature. To this institution they resolved to join the name of Elphinstone, in commememeration of the very valuable and praiseworthy efforts of that great and good man. This tribute of respect was at once gratifying to the heart of the gentleman to whom it was paid, and highly honourable to those from whom it emanated; while it also evidenced in a most graceful manner, the value the natives of Bombay set upon education.

In the year 1840 the two educational establishments were amalgamated under the designation of the Elphinstone Institution, by which name it is still known. This brief sketch of an institution, in the founding of which the Parsees had taken no insignificant part, and who of all the other races have derived the largest amount of benefit from it, is certainly not out of place here. Though the Hindoos* greatly outnumber the Parsees, the number of the latter who receive instruction at the Institution has always exceeded

* We leave out the Mahomedans altogether in our calculation, as they never trouble their heads about English education.

the former. In fact, the Parsees are the most intelligent and persevering of all the races inhabiting India, and it is only necessary for them to understand the value and benefits of that which is offered to them to induce them to grasp it with eagerness. This has been the case with English education. No Parsee, whose means can afford it, will neglect giving one to his children. The Elphinstone Institution swarms with Parsees; private schools, conducted by European gentlemen, are crowded with them; English and vernacular schools, established by Government in the different towns in the Mofussil are, wherever Parsees are to be found, chiefly resorted to by that race; indeed, the Parsees are mostly benefiting themselves by the education provided by the state.

If there is one fact more than another which can redound to the credit of this race, it is the enlightened manner in which the Parsees have recently viewed the question of education. They consider that the time has arrived when, independent of Governmental aid, they should provide for the education of their own people. In Bombay there is an institution superintended by a European professor, who has had considerable experience in the educational systems both of Europe and America, for the exclusive education of the Parsees. The name of this institution is not unfamiliar to those who have been in Bombay, or who have watched the progress of education in that presidency; we allude to the "Sir Jamsetjee Jeejeebhoy Parsee Benevolent Institution." As this institution is founded and entirely maintained by funds contributed by the Parsees, and especially by Sir Jamsetjee Jeejeebhoy, a short account of its origin and design may not be uninteresting.

In the year 1842, when Sir Jamsetjee Jeejeebhoy was raised to the dignity of knighthood, the Parsees were highly gratified at the mark of honour bestowed upon one of their number. They considered it their paramount duty to offer publicly their sincere congratulations to the man, who had, by his well-known public spirit and generous application of the means placed by Providence at his disposal, not only earned honour for himself but reflected credit on the race of which he was a member.

The Parsees accordingly presented a handsome testimonial to Sir Jamsetjee accompanied by an address, in which they said, "To commemorate this auspicious event, we request your permission to apply a sum of money which we have subscribed, in forming a fund to be designated 'Sir Jamsetjee Jeejeebhoy's Translation Fund,' and to be vested in trustees for the purpose of being appropriated in defraying the expenses of translating into the Guzerati language such books from the European and Asiatic languages, whether ancient or modern, as may be approved of by the committee, to be by them published and distributed gratis or at a low price among the Parsee community, in furtherance of the education of our people of which you have ever been a warm friend and zealous patron."

Sir Jamsetjee's reply to this address, fully explains the origin of the institution which now bears his illustrious name. He said:—"Nothing could please me more than the purposes to which you propose to devote the funds that have been subscribed. I shall ever wish my name to be connected with every endeavour to diffuse knowledge amongst our people; and the surest way to incite them to elevate and improve themselves, to fit them to appreciate the blessings of the Government under which they live, and to deserve those honours which have now, for the first time, been extended to India, is to spread far and wide amongst them, gratuitously, or in a cheap form, translations into our own language of the works of the most approved authors. Connected with this subject is a scheme that I have long contemplated, for relieving the distresses of the Parsee poor of Bombay, Surat, and its neighbourhood. You know full well the state of misery in which many of our people are living, and hopeless ignorance in which their children are permitted to grow up. My object is to create a fund, the interest of which shall be applied towards relieving the indigent of our people, and the education of their children, and I propose to invest the sum of 300,000 rupees in the public securities, and to place it at the disposal of trustees, who with the interest, shall carry out the object I have mentioned, and this trust I hope you will take under your care."

To this sum of 300,000 rupees, the munificent knight further added fifteen shares in the Bank of Bengal, Lady Jamsetjee five, and the Parsee punchayet thirty-five shares. This further contribution of fifty-five shares being valued at the time at three lacs and 96,000 rupees. The annual income of the institution, derived from the interest of the sum of three lacs of rupees, and dividend on the above mentioned shares amounts to 40,000 rupees.

The aggregate number of boys receiving instruction in the central and Mofussil schools of this institution, was at the date of the last report, 1,294. For the success and usefulness of the establishment Sir Jamsetjee has the best wishes of every Parsee.

In connection with the subject of education we must not omit to mention that there are now springing up several schools for the instruction of infants, on the plan adopted in the United Kingdom, and this system of early education is likely to be of much advantage in the mental training and in the formation of the moral habits of Parsee children.

In medical science, too, the Parsees have made considerable progress. The Grant Medical College has its fair proportion of Parsee students and graduates. One of them, as we have already mentioned, has competed successfully for a commission as assistant-surgeon in the Honourable Company's service. The reader will have observed from the foregoing pages, that the Parsees are now making a very fast run in the pursuit of knowledge. One clever Parsee, Mr. Dadabhai Naorosjee, was lately professor of mathematics and natural philosophy, in the Elphinstone Institution, while his general acquirements were known to be of a high order. Others were assistant-professors in the same institution. These undoubtedly are but a few instances, and we mention them to show that the favourable state of things which has now commenced, will in time be attended by the most happy results. Every day adds to the number seeking instruction in the literature of the West. Much good is expected from this thirst for knowledge, as the effect of English education upon the Parsees generally, will be to raise them still higher in the scale of civilization.

The history of female education among the Parsees, is very interesting. The first who appreciated its value, and endeavoured to introduce it into his own family, was the late lamented Framjee Cowasjee, Esq. The enterprising spirit, which had essayed the culture of silk and the manufacture of sugar, had observantly noted the effect of education upon European ladies. Where, then, could he introduce it more fittingly, and with greater promise of success, than in his own family? He, however, did not realize his best expectations, and the first experiment, owing to causes which need not be mentioned here, failed.

No other Parsee then thought of turning his attention to the culture of the female members of his family. From the failure of the first experiment, the wisdom of their ancestors in keeping females in a state of ignorance became manifest. The present Parsee Judge of the Court of Small Causes at Bombay, who had visited Europe, did not, however, share in the prejudices of his time. He, to his credit be it said, boldly opposed the popular prejudice, received with indifference and contempt the vulgar remarks of the ignorant, and commenced the education of his family in English.

The people generally thought that the utmost limit to which female education could extend was to teach their wives and daughters to scrawl letters, in order that they might be able to write a list of old clothes before sending them to the washerman or laundress; to understand the daily bazaar expenses, which, if they exceeded five rupees, would pass their limits of comprehension; and to read the name and residence of their husbands or fathers on a small bit of paper, which was sent from the market with the fuel or corn. These three acquirements of "reading, riting and rithmetic" were luxuries indeed, and the possessor was envied on account of her superior training!

A great change, however, soon took place. The young men who had been educated in Government schools and colleges viewed the question of female education in its proper light. They began to feel for the condition of their better halves. They plainly saw that their own domestic life could not be rendered happy if their wives remained uneducated, nor could the Parsee community generally be said to have advanced in a moral or social point of view if their women remained in a semi-barbarous state. They rightly understood that, if the seeds of education were to be generally spread, they should first germinate with the gentler sex. The influence which a mother or sister exercises upon a child was rightly conceived, and the enthusiastic youths determined to do some service to their country and countrymen, by earnestly directing their attention to the cause of female education.

The Students' Literary and Scientific Society* was the great medium for the exposition of the feelings and sentiments of

* The following, which we take from the address of Professor Reid, delivered at the annual exhibition of the distribu-

these young men. Here numerous essays on the social condition of the women of India

tion of prizes to the girls' school, explains the origin of this useful institution and its vernacular branches:—

"It was during the May vacation of 1848, two months after our arrival in Bombay, that my much-regretted friend, the late Professor Patton, and myself, determined to attempt something of this sort. There was then in a very languishing condition a sort of historical debating club called the Native Literary Society, where the merits of the 'dire Hannibal' and the guilt of Brutus were occasionally discussed. One visit to this society was enough to satisfy us of its utter want of adaptation, either to the necessities of the students, or to the position in which they stood with respect to their country. The question before the meeting was, 'Whether Cæsar was or was not a *great* man.' The champions of the affirmative had *read* their speeches on a former night, and their opponents now came forward with *written* answers, which were expected to provoke on some future occasion written rejoinders! In the place of this sickly exotic was fixed a plant more suited to the soil, which with tropical luxuriance grew up, in less than three years, into a goodly tree, beneath the wide-spreading branches of which hundreds of both sexes, adults as well as infants, were congregating to enjoy the life-bestowing fruits of knowledge.

"*Our First Session.*—It was proposed that the business of the new society should be conducted by the reading of essays on literary, scientific, and social subjects; and by discussing the topics introduced in a conversational manner. It was considered prudent not to open the society, at first, to others than professors, masters, students, and ex-students of the Elphinstone Institution; and also to exclude from the sphere of discussion all questions connected with the politics of the day, as well as all matters of religious controversy. At the close of the first session, in May, 1849, forty-six students—being double the number of the original members—were enrolled. Twenty meetings had been held, at which thirty-five essays were read were read, and the necessity of education as a means of raising them in the social

and discussed, most of the questions treated of being of a social character.

"*Vernacular Branches Organised.*—In September, 1848—three months after the foundation of the parent society—two vernacular branches were organised, under the Sanskrit appellation of *Dnyân-prasârak*, or knowledge-diffuser, and styled respectively *Marâthi* and *Gujarâti* from the language used by each as the medium of communication. The object proposed by their foundation was 'to promote the diffusion of knowledge among the uneducated masses, by the reading and discussing of essays on literary, historical, and social subjects; by lectures on physical and chemical science, accompanied by experiments; and by the publication of a cheap monthly periodical literature, suited to the requirements and tastes of the people." The nature of the connection which exists between these vernacular branches and the parent society is explained in the reports of the Managing Committee:—'In this society, all who become members are expected to contribute. They come here to give, as well as to receive, information. This is a Mutual Improvement Society. In the branch societies, the members of this society go out among their brethren as teachers. The knowledge which they discuss and digest here, they there convey, through the medium of a common language, to their less fortunate brethren, who have neither access to the walks of knowledge, nor time to devote to its pursuit."

"*Lectures on Popular Science.*—In those branch societies almost every topic of popular science has, in its turn, been lectured upon, illustrated with experiments, or otherwise familiarly expounded: the air-pump, the balloon, and the magic lantern—the mariner's compass, steam, and the electric telgraph—the properties of food, and the laws of health,

> 'And somewhat of the frame, the rock, the star;
> Electric, chemic laws; and all the rest.'

"*Discussion on Social Reform.*—Still more important in

scale was emphatically pointed out. Discussions on these subjects appeared in newspapers, magazines, and afterwards in lectures in the vernacular branches of the before mentioned society. The most sanguine of the educated Parsees never allowed any opportunity to be lost when they could sift the question of female education, and impress its advantages on the people.

Still nothing was practically done, excepting some isolated efforts made by a husband or

their effects are the teachings on social matters. It is proposed to discuss some favourite theme: let us suppose 'The advantages to be derived from foreign travel,' or 'The unhappy results of early marriages.' Notice of the debate is given in the daily or weekly newspapers, written in the language of the orators—newspapers of which the orators themselves, or their friends, are, in most cases, the editors. Four or five hundred individuals of various classes and creeds eagerly throng to listen. The discussion is conducted for hours; it has sometimes happened for consecutive meetings. The representative units of the unleavened masses listen, at first with astonishment, then with interest, and finally, let us hope, with delight and gratitude; and, when the meeting breaks up, return home to their respective circles, determined, as far as their influence and authority extend, to carry out the recommended reform."

The services this society has rendered to the natives of India are thus acknowledged by the Honourable the Court of Directors in their despatch to the Bombay Government:—

"We regard with special interest the efforts made by the Students' Literary and Scientific Society for the mental improvement of their countrymen and countrywomen."

brother to teach his wife or sister. The professors of the Elphinstone Institution, who were connected with the Students' Society, took great interest in the cause; and it must be mentioned that their encouragement and guidance mainly contributed to its success. The future generation of Parsee women will remember the names of Patton and Reid with gratitude and respect.

While the question was in the highest state of agitation in Bombay, a new stimulus came from an unexpected quarter. In Calcutta, about this time, the cause of female education was advocated with a spirit and eloquence quite unprecedented by the late Mr. Bethune, then law member of the Legislative Council of India, and his large-hearted munificence promised for Eastern India the commencement of a new era. In Bombay Mr. Bethune's exertions brought fresh moral strength, as many were anxiously waiting for a leader fortified with the prestige of rank, and possessing social and political influence.

Fortunately Parsee female education did not commence under such auspices. It might have thrown a bright light at the beginning, dazzled many, and attracted the people by the novelty; but with all these aids female education would have remained an exotic plant. There would have been wanting the stability and strength against accidents which are so conspicuous in an indigenous system.*

Education among the Parsee females cannot be said to have truly commenced until the latter end of the year 1849. To the society so frequently mentioned, the Parsees of Bombay are indebted for a systematic scheme for the education of their daughters. Numerous essays, which were read on the much-discussed subject, had prepared the

* "14. There is one point connected with the schools which we feel some delicacy in noticing; but as it is one concerning which the public press, while for the most part affording us the kindest and most flattering assistance, has fallen into some degree of error, we may perhaps be allowed to make a very cursory allusion to it. It has been assumed that the movement in the cause of female education which we sought to initiate was scarcely likely to succeed, unless assisted by the prestige of rank and of political and social influence. That prestige of this description is very powerful in India, it would of course be idle to dispute; but in the establishment of female schools the extremely sensitive prejudices which were to be encountered were evidently far less likely to take alarm at a project originating among the people themselves, and originally carried out by funds and by gratuitous teaching from the same quarter. And this too was the view taken by one of our daily papers, which observed, 'We must say, we think that the education of their females, which is undertaken by the natives themselves, is most likely to prosper.'"—*Second Annual Report of the Students' Literary and Scientific Society.*

minds of the hearers for action; and the last essay came in when every one was ready to commence the good work.* The evening on which that essay was read was the proudest in the history of the Students' Literary and Scientific Society. When the reading was concluded, the members present proceeded to the consideration of the measures for the consummation of their long-cherished desires.

They thought that there had been sufficient talking, and that the time had arrived for action, accordingly that evening the work was inaugurated. But could anything be done without pecuniary aid? This question was also easily solved. Several members of the society not only volunteered as teachers, but offered apartments in their own premises to serve as temporary schoolrooms. The hours of instruction were fixed from seven till ten A.M., that the other avocation of the volunteer teachers might not be interfered with.

* "Behramji's essay came in proper time. It was brimful of enthusiasm. His earnest appeal—accompanied, in the impressive oriental style, with a prayer to the Almighty—to do something, met with a hearty response. 'Let every student here present use his influence with the members of his own family to get one pupil at least.' 'Yes;' responded scores of voices. 'Let us teach the schools ourselves, and show that we are in earnest.' 'Yes! yes!' exclaimed all."—*Report of the Students' Literary and Scientific Society for* 1854-55.

Under this arrangement four Parsee girls' schools were opened on the 22nd of October, 1849, and forty-four pupils attended on the first day.* For six months instruction was given

* The following circular drawn up by Professor Patton, briefly explains the nature of the instruction which it was proposed should be imparted at the schools:—

"The members of the Students' Literary and Scientific Society, deeply impressed with the necessity of female education, and anxious to contribute, as far as in their power, to its dissemination among the people of this country, have established seven girls' schools, from the 1st October last.

"The Society is anxious to draw the attention of those parents who have already promised to send their children, and of such as may still wish for further information, to the following particulars regarding the schools; and they feel confident, that the character of the teachers, and the nature of the education to be communicated, will command the sympathy and support of all who are interested in the regeneration of India.

"It is usual in elementary schools to teach only reading and writing; but these, although important as contributing to future progress, have no influence on the moral and intellectual nature, and consequently have little title to the name of education.

"In the schools of the Society the chief attention will be given to the culture of the moral nature, under which is included the formation of habits of order, propriety, and cleanliness; and this is proposed to be effected chiefly by means of moral tales read by the masters, which will interest the children. In the mental culture, every effort will be made to form habits of observation by means of lessons on familiar objects, such as animals, trees, &c.; and the Society hope that in a short time they will have attached to each school a small museum and a collection of pictures, which will cultivate not only the senses, but also the taste."

in these schools by the volunteer teachers, and well and creditably did they perform their self-imposed task. The following eulogy was passed upon their labours in a late report of the society :—

"The prudence and caution which these youthful reformers displayed in applying themselves to the laborious details of their self-imposed task, were as admirable as the generous enthusiasm which sustained them throughout its performance. Carefully did they prepare themselves for their duties, by reading every work on practical education within their reach, and by holding frequent meetings to consider how they might best instruct the children that were entrusted to their care. Their design was not simply to teach reading and writing, but to give such an education as would have an influence on the whole character."

The schools firmly established, the advantages resulting therefrom were at once perceived by those who visited them. The efficient practical working of the schools made a stronger impression on the minds of the people than the mere talk of years. Men not wanting in liberality of sentiment, and ready of purse, now came forward to assist in the good and noble cause which a few youthful reformers had undertaken with so much credit to themselves. The first pecuniary aid received towards the maintenance of the schools was from four Parsee gentlemen, whose names, at their special request, were not publicly given out at the time, for they loved to do good "by stealth, and blushed to find it fame." Latterly, however, these names transpired, and they are well worth preserving in these pages as those of the first Parsees through whose pecuniary assistance, so seasonably given, the girls' schools of their community were commenced on something like a solid foundation. Hope was now brightened for the success and duration of the schools.

Messrs. Nusserwanjee Muncheejee Cama, Framjee Nusserwanjee Patel, Dhungheebhoy Nusserwanjee Cama, and Cursetjee Nusserwanjee Cama, were the liberal gentlemen who performed the good work. They placed at the disposal of the Committee a sum of 4,800 rupees, to be expended in maintaining the schools then opened for a period of two years; at the expiration of which time it was thought "the public would not willingly let them die."

The benefits arising from the schools were

now fully appreciated by the Parsees: the number attending them in the second year of their establishment greatly exceeded that in the first year. The European residents of the place also began to take a warm interest in the undertaking. Men like Sir Erskine Perry, the indefatigable President of the late Board of Education, and many other influential gentlemen, not only interested themselves in the promotion of the object by presenting liberal donations, but by their advice and encouragement greatly contributed to the success of the scheme.

In the second year of their foundation these schools were viewed in the light of valuable public institutions. Their progress and success were watched with peculiar interest, and the care and prudence with which their affairs were managed by the society which founded them, afforded an additional security towards the accomplishment of the great end for which they were brought into being. In the year 1851 the Government of Lord Falkland regarded the spontaneous institution of these schools "as an epoch in the history of education in the Bombay Presidency, from which, it was hoped, would in due time be traced the commencement of a rapid, marked, and constant progress."*

One of the great drawbacks to the spread of female education at present is, that the girls are generally removed from the schools

* The following, which we extract from Professor Sinclair's address to the Right Hon. the Governor, who presided at a late exhibition of these schools, will give an idea of the nature of the instruction imparted to pupils at the female schools:—

"The children are taught exclusively in their vernacular languages. The following books have been prepared both in the Gujarati and the Marathi, with the exception of Æsop's Fables, which as yet is confined to Marathi schools:—Dnyanbodhak, parts 1 and 2; Moral Class Book; Major Candy's Vernacular Reader, Balmitra, Arithmetic as far as fractions. Moral tales taken chiefly from English books, are conveyed by their masters in the vernacular languages to the children; these tales, a few days after, the children repeat to the master, when they have been for a little while in the alembic of their own thought; this is a very excellent exercise, it engages their interest and cultivates at the same time the memory and the affections, and their general intelligence. Garbas or songs of a moral nature are sung by them in the way of recreation; these are chanted in the anthem or responsive manner, generally, with a good deal of spirit, but with a deficiency of taste and intonation. To proceed to the external world:—they have lessons on the surrounding objects—'What is the table made of?' 'How was the copper-pot made?' 'Whence did the copper come?' 'Why is the copper-pot tinned?' &c. They have pictures to illustrate natural history and the trades. There have been also lately received wooden figures of various quadrupeds and birds. Their domestic industry so far consists of sewing, working in Berlin wool, and of embroidering; habits of cleanliness, order, regularity and truth are habitually inculcated."

between the ages of ten and twelve. This is owing to early marriages and the prejudices still existing against allowing grown up girls to attend schools entirely conducted, superintended, and planned by *men*. So long as the places of teachers are not supplied by females, there is little hope that girls will be allowed to continue their stay at the schools to a more advanced age.

To meet this difficulty a class of qualified native female teachers is essential, and the subject has already engaged the attention of the committee. One girl, we are happy to say, is now mistress in one of the schools. She owes her education entirely to the school over which she now proudly presides. This is a beginning of the most important kind; and when the number of such teachers shall have multiplied, one great obstacle to the furtherance of the noble cause will have been removed.

Every encouragement to induce girls to continue at the schools with the view of qualifying themselves for the post of teacher, is held out. At the last exhibition, the President of the Society announced that a noble-minded Parsee gentleman had signified his intention of bestowing annually a prize of

500 rupees upon the best qualified pupil in the girls' schools, who may be found willing to conduct a school as teacher for a period of not less than three years."*

If so much has been accomplished by a society of young men, much is expected from the new impetus that has lately been given to this cause. The Parsee community can now be said to be entirely agreed as regards the necessity of female education. Some of the most influential and leading members of the body have very recently resolved upon a plan for the extension and entire re-organization of the schools.

After thanking the members of the Students'

* In the year 1853, Professor Reid, President of the Students' Society threw out a suggestion by which female education may be continued to a very advanced age, if not in the schools, at least in the children's own houses. He advised the publication, and at first the gratis distribution of entertaining monthly miscellanies in the vernacular language of the children, and specially adapted to the capacity and taste of those young girls who yearly leave the schools, with sufficient preliminary instructions to profit by such a publication. The idea was good, but was not adopted till the commencement of last year, when a cheap monthly publication of thirty pages, the size of the Family Herald, at a cost of a rupee per annum was commenced, containing articles on various subjects likely to interest female readers. The circulation of this periodical within a year of its starting reached 1,500 copies; a number unprecedentedly large among any one class of native readers.

Society for what has already been achieved through their agency, these gentlemen requested them to transfer the schools to their charge, and offered to provide ample funds for their permanent maintenance. The society cordially acceded to their request, and our European readers, by whom the value and blessings of female education cannot be better appreciated, will be rejoiced to learn, that in addition to the funds which the above-mentioned Society made over to schools, no less than 15,000 rupees were subscribed in a few days.* We can now fairly say that as the Parsees themselves have undertaken the education of their females, it is most likely to go

* We here subjoin the names of such as have subscribed 500 rupees and upwards.

	Rupees.
Framjee Nusserwanjee, Esq.	2,000
Manockjee Nusserwanjee, Esq.	1,000
Cursetjee Nusserwanjee Camajee, Esq.	1,000
Byramjee Jeejeebhoy, Esq.	1,000
Bomonjee Framjee Camajee, Esq.	1,000
Dhunjeebhoy Nusserwanjee Camajee, Esq.	1,000
Jehanjee Nusserwanjee Wadia, Esq.	1,000
Soonabai, widow of Nusserwanjee Muncherjee Camajee, Esq.	1,000
Pestonjee Framjee Camajee, Esq.	500
Dosabhoy Framjee Camajee, Esq.	500
Dosabhoy Hormusjee Camajee, Esq.	500
Pestonjee Hormusjee Camajee, Esq.	500
Sorabjee Pestonai, Esq.	500

on and prosper. The schools have now taken a natural and firm root, and promise a permanent existence.

With prospects so brilliant before us, it is right to confess that female education among the Parsees is still in its infancy. Much is expected when girls' schools shall have multiplied, with a good staff of female teachers. At present there are seven * Parsee girls' schools in Bombay, attended by 1,000 girls. According to a late census, there are 12,000 Parsee female children under the age of fourteen. The average age of leaving school is eleven, and the pupils commence the attendance at four, so that it will be seen a very large percentage of the Parsee girls are receiving instruction.

We fervently hope, that with the increasing sense of the responsibility of educating females, and the great encouragement and pp o rt the scheme receives from all quarters, the Parsee females of a quarter of a century hence, will rise far superior in intellect to their sisters of preceding generations. We trust, too, they will not only become better wives and

* This number includes the three schools established in connection with the Sir Jamsetjee Jeejeebhoy's Parsee Benevolent Institution.

better mothers, but by their mental qualifications and advanced position exercise a great influence on the future moral and social advancement of their race.

That education has and will exercise great influence on the Parsees is a fact not to be controverted. The difference between the Parsees of thirty years ago and those of the present day, is simply the result of English education and intercourse with Englishmen. The question may perhaps be asked, how many Parsees have received what might be called a sound education? Not many, we freely admit, comparing the number educated to the whole mass, but we unhesitatingly assert that the example and influence of the few, have worked wonderful changes on the minds of the many.

Our educated men have, almost without exception, been remarkable for the purity of their conduct, while the disinterestedness of their views, their honesty of purpose, their love for the good of their countrymen, and their high moral courage, have been the theme of universal praise. To spread generally among their less fortunate brethren that enlightenment and knowledge which they have received through the means provided by a beneficent

Government, has been their constant aim and the highest object of their ambition.

A noble band of educated Parsees have within the last few years, by the publication of cheap newspapers * or magazines, or by public lectures, all more or less calculated to impart information and knowledge to the mass, worked such an extraordinary change on the character of their race, that whatever we could say in praise of the exertions of the

* There are fourteen newspapers published in the Guzerati language, which are mostly circulated among the Parsees. Three of them are published daily, one tri-weekly, three bi-weekly, six weekly, and one fortnightly. The *Rast-Goftar*, a weekly newspaper, is the most influential and best of all. It enjoys the largest circulation, is conducted by the most talented men of the community, and always represents the sentiments and feelings of the educated, liberal-minded, and enlightened portion of the population. It deals, we may say without fear of contradiction, with public men and public measures in a pungency of style and independence of tone at least equal to that of its English brethren on the spot. To this paper is undeniably due the credit of having greatly contributed, by the force and weight of its vigorous articles, to the abolition of many superstitions practised among the natives, and the introduction of reforms calculated to raise the moral and social condition of the people to a higher scale of civilization. The daily papers are also creditably conducted. Of the bi-weekly journals the *Chabook* is the best, and is one of the most spirited native journals in India. The *Suttaya Prakash*, a journal circulated chiefly among the Hindoo portion of the population of Bombay, is a very clever paper indeed, and is expected to do that service to the Hindoos which the *Rast-Goftur* has done to the Parsees.

youthful innovators, would be inadequate to express our sense of what they have done. We are content to say that they have fully succeeded in awakening in the minds of their countrymen the necessity of a general and rapid advancement in the path of knowledge and enlightenment, if they desire to be classed among the civilized nations of the earth.

In this spirit the Parsees are now acting, and if it should happen to continue, another age, will, under God's blessing, produce no insignificant results. Even to-day, those seeking instruction and enlightenment are not confined to the walls of the schools. At the meeting of the literary societies, at public lectures, and at libraries, large numbers of Parsees are always to be seen gathering information in every shape and from whatever source it can be obtained.

It has hitherto been a just subject for reproach, that our wealthy families pay less attention to the education of their youths than they ought to do; those hitherto extensively benefiting by English education belonging to the middle class. We cannot say whether this remark will stand good any longer, as indeed some change for the better has already taken place. The rich have seen that wealth will not be the only qualification for maintaining their position in society. They have perceived that if they do not leave for their sons a better legacy than gold, they will be thrown overboard in society, and the educated and enlightened members of the middle or less wealthy classes will take precedence of them in every way. Such a result would be inevitable, if the rich Parsees still neglected to educate their families in a manner befitting their position. But we are not doomed to this, since matters are mending in this respect.

As one example does more in bringing about a desirable effect than a hundred precepts, one or two instances have in some measure contributed towards creating a taste for study among our wealthier class, and we think we may with justice notice them here. Mr. Sorabjee Jamsetjee, the youngest son of Sir Jamsetjee, though he bids fair to walk in the general footsteps of his venerable parent, has distinguished himself in a new sphere of usefulness. He is a member of the Bombay Branch of the Royal Asiatic Society, and has an extraordinary taste for the study of languages. He has given to the world three works in the vernacular language of the country, showing an extensive acquaintance with Oriental literature. These were not published by him with a view to pecuniary profit. Providence has favoured him with abundance, and one of the best uses he made of his money was to distribute the works, of which thousands of copies were struck off, gratis among the people.

A gentleman of extended and liberal views, greatly in advance of his other rich brethren, Mr. Sorabjee Jamsetjee is always ready to assist, by the prestige of his wealth and influence, any undertaking which may have for its object the welfare of his countrymen. Himself a man of high moral conduct, he is always ready to preach to others what he himself practises. On a late occasion, he did not think it beneath his dignity to deliver a public lecture on "human life, its duties and responsibilities."* Such was the estimation

* The following notice of the lecture is taken from the *Bombay Times*:—

"The lecture delivered by Mr. Sorabjee Jamsetjee in the Council-room of the Town Hall, on Thursday evening, the 27th March, 1856, a sketch of which will be found in another column, was one of extreme interest both in a social and ethical point of view. It was in the Guzerati language, the vernacular tongue of the people of his tribe, the Parsee, but interspersed with many quotations from English, Persian, and other languages, which were uniformly correctly translated for the benefit of the audience. It was entirely of a moral character, dealing with the responsibility of man to God, the importance in which the lecture was held, that the Town Hall, where it was delivered, was literally crammed to excess. From the millionaire to the poorest man, from the most learned to the humblest student, every one was present to listen to the oratory and sentiments of the Parsee baronet's son. After the lecture, the Rev. Dr. Wilson, head missionary of the Free Church of Scotland, and several other European and native speakers, bore testimony to the ability and eloquence with which it was delivered.

Mr. Sorabjee Jamsetjee has thus set a valuable example to his wealthy brethren, and

of life in relation to eternity, the necessity of preparation for death, and the final judgment which awaits every individual of the human race. It appropriately and strikingly illustrated the primary and essential duties of man to himself, to his fellows, and to his Maker, its whole aim being to induce every member of the community to live soberly, righteously, and godly. It may be safely asserted that seldom has such an excellent discourse been delivered to such a large assembly of natives in Bombay, comprising about six or seven hundred of the most influential classes of society of all sects and ages. With a very few alterations it might have done for the Christian pulpit. We are glad to hear that it will immediately obtain publicity through the press. It will convince multitudes that the Jamsetjee family is illustrious not only for princely almsgiving, but for the most commendable philanthropic action. The Mobeds will see from it that they must either soon amend their teaching or have their services dispensed with altogether."

shown that advancement in learning is not incompatible with business in public life, and that wealth without wisdom is but a poor satisfaction to its possessor. He has engaged a European teacher for the instruction of his sons in the science and literature of Europe.

Another gratifying instance of a son of a rich man devoting himself to study, and benefiting his countrymen by the light of his own knowledge, while also engaged in extensive business transactions, deserves notice. Mr. Dhunjeebhoy Framjee, a son of Shet, Framjee Nusserwanjee, and partner in the firm of Messrs. Wallace and Co., at Bombay, has long been distinguished as an Oriental scholar. He, too, is a member of the Bombay branch of the Royal Asiatic Society, and at one of its meetings read a very interesting paper on the "origin and authenticity of the Iranian family of languages." About two years since, he published a grammar of the Huzwaresh or Pehlvi proper, which was highly spoken of, and favourably reviewed by the Press.

Mr. Dhunjeebhoy Framjee has been engaged for many years on a most laborious but useful task, that of compiling a dictionary of Zend, Pehlvi, and English terms, and his countrymen look forward to its publication with intense interest. This work will be an invaluable addition to the literature of the East, which has now engaged the attention of some of the best of our continental scholars.

We have also much pleasure in recording in these pages the fact, that four Parsee students, sons of rich Parsee merchants of Bombay, are now receiving education at the University College, London. The advantages which will result are obvious, and the benefits these young gentlemen will derive from their education in England, will, no doubt, stimulate others to follow their example.

We trust the example thus set to the younger members of our wealthy families, will be generally followed, and we fondly hope that the future historian of the Parsees will be able to make honourable mention of hundreds of instances of this kind. In the meantime we cannot do better than recommend to the attention of such of our countrymen who, by the possession of riches, either think lightly of the pursuit of knowledge, or unjustly urge against its continuance, after they have left the walls of the school or college, on the score of active professional or business occupation, the following sentiments of the late Professor Forbes of Edinburgh.

"Plausible as this objection seems, it is not well founded. The proof that it is not so lies in the fact that many of the ablest professors of natural history, as well as of other sciences, and I may add, of literature and philosophy, are men diligently engaged in daily duties of a different kind, and doing their tasks thoroughly and well. The names of many of the most eminent of British men of science are those of fully occupied physicians and successful merchants. In the last century, Ellis, a busy London merchant, changed the whole face of zoophytology. Only last year died Charles Stokes, a name not popularly known, but very familiar to men of science at home and abroad, similarly occupied with Ellis, who, nevertheless, found time to aid, by his extensive original knowledge and ever judicious advice, almost every naturalist of whatever denomination in Europe. At the present moment I could point out several of our very best zoologists and geologists among the most diligent and ablest of British merchants. Let it not be pleaded, then, that science and literature are to be put aside on account of active professional occupations of any kind. The excuse never comes from the able and willing. It is exactly by the aid of the classes of men who do their professional and business duties best that science and literature have reaped, and are reaping, their most valuable interests."

Of all the natives of India the Parsees are undoubtedly the most loyal subjects of the British Government. Their loyalty is not one of empty show, nor the result of a fear of a strong and powerful government, but is the offspring of deep-rooted conviction. When they compare their condition in India with that of their co-religionists in Persia, who are reduced to the most miserable state by misgovernment and persecution, they fully and rightly appreciate the blessings which they enjoy under this Government. When they see that for more than full ten centuries they had to drag on in misery and poverty under the native rulers of India, and their own enterprise or spirit could bring them no reward; bearing all this in mind, when they reflect upon their present prosperous condition, and inquire into its causes, they find abundant reasons to pray that the Sovereignty, which the Almighty God in the wise dispensation of his Providence has been pleased to place over them, may be for ever preserved.

Whenever fitting opportunities have occurred, the Parsees have not forgotten or neglected to show this love towards their rulers. When the British Government appointed a day of humiliation and prayer for the speedy restoration of peace and success to the arms of England and France during the late war with Russia, the Parsees behaved themselves as the most worthy subjects of the British Crown. In a highly loyal spirit they made arrangements for the observance of that day according to the invitation of their much-respected Government. No less than 6,000 of this race met together in one of their fire-temples, for the purpose of offering their prayers for the success of the Allied Powers and the restoration of peace. In the following prayer, which was prepared for the occasion, the rich and the poor alike joined with heart and soul:

"I offer my prayer to Thee, O glorious and exalted God, that the Sovereign of this realm may gain the victory with honour and triumph in the war. May the Sovereign of sovereigns inspire with wisdom and endow with strength her army and navy. Long live the Sovereign, and may the empire flourish. May God annihilate her enemies, and may His blessing rest upon her. May He watch over all the events, and destroy the enemy. I make my prayer and supplications unto

Thee, Almighty God, that success may attend the cause of our Queen in the field of battle. May our Queen continue her rule in justice and mercy, and may her name and her power be handed down to many generations. May she ever maintain in all its integrity her exalted position, which is illumined with light and glory. Such is my prayer.—Amen."

To show how sincere the Parsees were in what they were doing, it must be mentioned that, previous to the prayer, they performed certain religious ceremonies, similar to those which the ancient Zoroastrians were in the habit of performing when their own monarchs were engaged in formidable wars against their enemies. At this day the Parsees acknowledge Her Most Gracious Majesty, the Queen of England, as their lawful Sovereign, and they therefore feel no hesitation in doing that for their present government which their forefathers were wont to do for their ancient Kings.

When a day was appointed, on the capture of Sebastopol, for a general thanksgiving to the Almighty, the Parsees again performed a similar ceremony, and we here give a translation of the prayer which was compiled for the occasion, as it not only shows the feeling and spirit of the Parsees in the brightest light, but strongly displays their appreciation of the Government under which they live.

"O Almighty God, let Thy shadow always fall wherever the British rule exists. Grant it, O God, success in all its undertakings; vanquish by the aid of Thy powerful hands all its enemies, and grant that its greatness may still rise, and its moral effects be spread over a still greater portion of the world. Receive our humble acknowledgments, O Lord, for having placed us under such a beneficent rule, and we pray to Thee to preserve us under it. Grant, O Heaven, that the Government over our head, be actuated in ruling over us, with still greater kindness, and its effects be spread still wider. O Almighty Protector, preserve for ever secure our lives and properties, as they now are—and grant that the security may be still more strengthened. Bestow, O Lord, a still more merciful heart to the Queen who reigns over us. We pray to Thee, O Almighty God, to bless her armies with success in the great war in which they are now engaged, and bring to a speedy termination the great strife, by granting victory to those who have gone to shed their blood in the right cause. Grant, O Gracious God, that we may continue to live, as we now do, with perfect security to ourselves under the Government in which we now are, and that we may ever be impressed with a grateful sense of the advantages which we enjoy under this benign reign. Amen."

We may add, that similar proceedings were instituted by this loyal race on the final termination of the great war. In connection with this subject, we reproduce here the speech of Sir Jamsetjee Jeejeebhoy, delivered on the occasion of the "Patriotic Fund" meeting in the Town Hall of Bombay (January 3rd, 1855). Though the interest of the war has long since paled, we are anxious to record in these pages, the views and feelings of the Parsees in India in regard to it. We have no doubt that even at this distant day, the speech will be read with interest by the European community, as the unprejudiced voice of the natives of India on a subject, which had so lately engaged the attention of the whole civilized world. The reader is requested particularly to mark the venerable Parsee's love for the Queen. Addressing Lord Elphinstone, who had presided on the occasion, Sir Jamsetjee said,—

"My lord,—Under the weight of years I am unable to take that active part in aid of the Patriotic Fund which it has hitherto been my greatest happiness to take in promoting the benevolent enterprises of the day. I felt all the more desirous, therefore, to assure your lordship and the community of my most cordial and unqualified sympathy with this great movement. My lord, when I consider that the principle of this meeting, convened in answer to your lordship's call, is pure benevolence, I cannot repress the desire which I feel to have a voice in it; and as I am prevented by the infirmities of age from personally addressing so large an audience, I would solicit the favour of being permitted to address the meeting by the mouth of a beloved son."

Mr. Sorabjee Jamsetjee then said,—"My lord, with your lordship's kind permission, I beg most respectfully to communicate to your lordship and the gentlemen of Bombay here assembled, the views and feelings of my venerable father in reference to the deeply affecting and interesting occasion and object of this meeting.

"My lord and gentlemen, I should not be able to offer any apology for addressing you, if I did so in the feeling that I had a right to demand your attention to my own personal sentiments on the subject which has brought you together. But if I endeavour, in the few remarks I have the honour to offer, to make you acquainted with the sentiments of the most reflecting portion of the Parsee community on this subject, I trust that you will not consider any apology necessary, but that I shall perform an acceptable service. My lord, I am sure all must feel that great seriousness becomes such a meeting as the present. Of none of the great evils which afflict our race do we form such inadequate conceptions as of the evils of war. War is exhibited to us in the dazzling dress of poetry, fiction and history, where its horrors are carefully concealed beneath its gaudy trappings; or we see, perhaps, its plumes and epaulettes, and harlequin finery, we hear of the magnificence of the apparatus, the bravery of the troops, the glory of the victors, but the story of the wholesale miseries and wretchedness, and wrongs which follow in its train, is untold.

"What nation is not groaning under war-debts, the greatest of national burdens! Had the inconceivable sum wasted in the work of human butchery, been applied to promote individual comfort and national prosperity, the world would not now be so far behind as it is in its career of progress. But if the earth has always groaned under the pecuniary expense of war, how much more deeply, in a different sense, has it groaned under the expense of human life incurred in war. It is estimated that not less than eighteen times the present population of the globe have perished in war. Oh! what lamentations and wailings of heart-broken widows and helpless orphans, and destitute old age, have been caused by the butchery of so many husbands, fathers, and sons.

"While all confess, however, that war is an evil, we must consider that it may be a necessary evil, and if necessary, then justifiable. I believe, my lord, that there is but one feeling in the Parsee community regarding the justice of the war which Britain is now waging. There is not one among us who agrees with John Bright, that 'the present war is the wickedest in which Great Britain ever was engaged.' No, my lord, we all feel that there never was, in the history of the world, a more honourable spectacle than that which has been exhibited by the British and French nations—the arms of Britain and France raised in combat for the purpose not only of supporting the weak against the strong, but of supporting the sacred principles of international right, the violation of which would have turned the world upside down—the arms of Britain and France raised in combat, not seeking conquests for selfish objects, but for those of the most noble and generous character—for the peace of the world, for the progress of civilization, and for the interests of freedom. Truly has it been said, that, 'in the great European movement towards free institutions which has been the keynote of history since 1815, Russia has always headed the party of absolutism and reaction. The whole weight of the Russian monarch has been thrown into the scale of despotism; his aid has always been ready to put down liberty, and it has been rendered with an unscrupulous and conscientious zeal.' And the position of Russia, my lord, more than that of any Government in existence, or that ever existed, puts tremendous evil in her power, unless the mercy of the Almighty shall check it by the arms of Britain and France. She is the only power which has partially the command of two land-locked seas. By her diplomacy directed against Denmark, and her arms directed against Turkey, she has been trying to get full possession of these seas. Had she succeeded, her fleets would soon have swept the ocean, and ravaged the world. She has betrayed her diabolical designs, and she will now be deprived, I trust, of both the Baltic and Black seas. Her diabolical designs! Yes; the last mail brought us the Czar's manifesto, in which he expounds his policy, and the object which Russia seeks to attain by the present war, and that object is to put down Britain, and the free government which Britain is extending over the earth. Such is the plain avowal of the Czar.

"My lord, our duty to relieve the sufferers in this great war would have remained the same whether the war had been a just one or not; but, considering the nature and objects of this war, we extend this relief now more as a privilege than as a duty. There is a luxury at any time in relieving the sufferings of the broken-down soldier who has manfully and bravely fought the battles of his country, or in alleviating the grief of the soldier's desolate widow and fatherless children; but there is a peculiar bliss in doing it on such an occasion as the present. My lord, I must adopt as my own language on this occasion the memorable words of Sir John McNeill:—'I trust that all those who have the means will feel that this is an opportunity of exercising a privilege.

It is an opportunity which I, for one, am determined not to be deprived of. I care not whether the funds are to be raised by taxation or otherwise. I claim for myself the privilege of gratifying my own feelings, by contributing to the alleviation of their sufferings. I reserve to myself the right of exercising my own benevolence by contributing to alleviate the distress of the families of those whose death we glory in as an honour to their country.'

"'Breathe all thy minstrelsy, immortal Harp!
Breathe numbers warm with love, while I rehearse
Thy praise, O Charity! thy labours, most
Divine; thy sympathy with sighs, and tears,
And groans; thy great, thy godlike wish, to heal
All misery, all Fortune's wounds, and make
The soul of every living thing rejoice.
Oh! thou wast needed much in days of Time!
No virtue, half so much; none half so fair!
To all the rest, however fine, thou gavest
A finishing and polish, without which
No man e'er entered heaven.'"

"Moreover, my lord, the Queen has made an appeal to us, and it is our duty to respond to it. I cannot refrain from eulogizing our gracious Queen. Religious Sovereigns are scattered at distant intervals along the centuries of the world's history, like 'angels' visits, few and far between.' In all this dreary length of way, they appear like five or six lighthouses on as many thousand miles of coast. But, my lord, the greatest nation now on earth is favoured with the best of earthly Sovereigns. The present appeal of her gracious Majesty is dictated by her pious heart; and I must say in reference to it, in the language of another: 'I should just as soon expect to see British soldiers refuse to bear their share in the storming of Sebastopol, because they did not approve of the general plan of the siege, as to find men who call themselves leal-hearted subjects, hesitate to meet this otherwise irresistible call, because the mode in which it is proposed to achieve the object, jars somewhat unpleasantly with their preconceived notions of Political Economy.'

"To the call of our Gracious Sovereign, and to the call of humanity, the Parsees, my lord, will cordially respond."

When the late unhappy revolt broke out in the upper provinces of India, the Parsees had further opportunities of displaying their loyalty to their rulers. They embraced the first that offered of presenting an address to his Lordship, the Governor, assuring him of their loyalty and attachment to the British Government, and offering their services in whatever way they might be required in suppressing the mutinies.

So great and well-known has been the loyalty of the Parsees, that while all the other races were, after the commencement of the rebellion, looked upon with distrust, not even a breath of suspicion was directed against the Parsees. Every European and the whole of the English Press acknowledged that this race would never be inimical to British rule. The best and most convincing proof of the loyalty of the Parsees will be found in the fact that, if there was any individual of this sect at any station where the revolt occurred, he suffered equally with the Europeans at the hands of the rebels, his sympathy with the Government being so well known.

If, unhappily, a disturbance ever occurred in Bombay the Europeans and Parsees of the place would be in one common boat, the latter being so well known to be in the interest of the present rulers, and to have no sympathy either with the Hindoos or Mahomedans. We do not think we need say more on a subject in which our sentiments are shared to the fullest extent by every Englishman in India, and by all those in England who have any knowledge of the character of the different races inhabiting that peninsula.

CHAPTER VII.

RELIGION.

The antiquity of the Parsee religion—Identity of Zoroaster—Birth of the Parsee prophet—His persecutions—Progress of Zoroastrianism—The Zend language—The Avasta—The fragments of the Avasta in the possession of modern Parsees—Disputes as to the liturgical works of the Parsees—Nature of the Parsee religion—Fire the emblem of the Almighty—The Parsees not worshippers of the elements—Ardai Veraf's vision—Religious reform—Education of Parsee priests.

THE faith professed by the Parsees in India is one of the most ancient. As we have shown, it was once the religion of the most famous empire of the world. It has had its day of greatness as well as of decline, and has during a period of twenty-four centuries undergone various persecutions and vicissitudes. From the time it was founded, in the reign of Gushtasp, or Darius Hystaspes, till the conquest of Persia by Alexander the Great, a period of three hundred years, it was in its most flourishing condition, the envious Greek having, it is said, destroyed a great many of the religious books of the Parsees.

For a period of five hundred and fifty-six years after the subversion of the Persian dynasty by the Macedonian Conqueror, the religion of Zoroaster seems to have declined, until revived by Ardeshir Babekan in A.D. 226. In the reign of this monarch great efforts were made for restoring its primitive purity, according to the doctrines propounded by Zoroaster, it having been greatly corrupted during the period above mentioned. The king himself was a person of great piety and religious enthusiasm. He collected the sacred books of the Parsees and had them translated into Pehlvi, the language then current in Persia, built fire-temples for the worship of God, and restored the ancient religion of Persia to its original and pure state. This reformation by Ardeshir Babekan seems to have lasted for a period of four hundred and sixteen years, indeed until the religion and monarchy of Persia were overthrown by the Arab invaders in the year 641.

There is some dispute, even now, among the Parsees as to the exact date of the birth of Zurtosht. European authors are in doubt as to whom to select of the half-dozen philosophers who, at different times, bore the name of Zoroaster, as the lawgiver of the Parsees. One is described as a Chaldean or Assyrian, one as a Bactrian, another as a Pamphylian; a fourth as an Armenian, and, lastly, one as a Persian.

Sir William Ouseley, in his valuable and well-known travels in Persia, is of opinion "that the prophet or legislator whose name we find written in Persian books Zerdehust or Zaratusht, is manifestly that Zoroaster whom the Greek historian Agathias calls Zoroados or Zarades, and justly assigns to the age of King Hystaspes, preceding Christ by about five hundred years." Mr. Nourozjee Furdoonjee, a learned Parsee of Bombay, a man of great research and undoubted ability, one of the companions of Sir Alexander Burnes in his second mission to Cabool, and now holding the position of translator and interpreter in her Majesty's Supreme Court at Bombay, in a work published by him in the year 1851, and entitled "Tareekh-i-Zurtoshtee; or, Discussion on the Era of Zurtosht or Zoroaster," has proved, to the satisfaction, it is believed, of the majority of the Parsees, by the testimony of Greek, Latin, French, English, and other European, as well as Pehlvi, Arabic, and

Persian authors of ancient and modern times, that Zurtosht flourished in the sixth century before the Christian era. Hyde, Prideaux, Anquetil, Kluker, Herder, Gorres, Von Hammer, Malcolm, De Gaigniant Kalprath, and others, have also adopted the view that places Zoroaster in the reign of Darius Hystaspes, in the sixth century before Christ.

The lawgiver of the Parsees, Zurtosht, Zerdusht, Zeratusht, or Zoroaster, as he is variously styled, was born at the city of Rai in Persia, and flourished in the reign of King Gushtasp, who embraced and propagated the faith propounded by him. One Poroshusp, remarkable for the uprightness of his life, was selected by God to be the father of the prophet. In Pehlvi works, originally compiled by the disciples of Zurtosht, it is said that an angel presented Poroshusp with a glass of wine; having drunk which, his wife Doghdo soon after conceived and bore a son, destined to create a new era in Eastern history. The circumstance of Zurtosht's father having received wine from an angel was publicly talked about, and the governor of the province resolved, at the instigation of wicked counsellors, to destroy the infant. The hands of the destroyers are said to have been, in every attempt for its destruction, arrested by divine agency.

While yet a child, he was subjected to no ordinary persecutions. He was, it is said, cast into blazing fire, but came out unscathed. He was once taken into a narrow lane where the oxen were accustomed to pass, that he might be trampled to death when the brutes came that way, but he remained unhurt. The same result ensued when he was thrown in the way of wolves and other wild beasts of the forest. Other instances of his escapes from the machinations of those in authority are related, but need not be repeated here, as at last he was allowed to remain unmolested.

In the Pehlvi books still existing, and originally compiled by the disciples of Zurtosht, the Persian Prophet, at the age of thirty, is said to have left his native town of Rai, and to have proceeded with all the members of his family to the capital of Persia. In the fortieth year of his age, and in the thirtieth of the reign of Gushtasp, he is reported to have appeared at the court of the King, bearing with him, into his presence, the sacred fire called "Ader Boorzeen Meher," and a cypress tree. The monarch having demanded who he was and whence he came, the Persian lawgiver replied, "The Almighty God has sent me to you, and has appointed me a prophet to guide you in the path of truth, virtue, and piety."

Firdousi, the Persian Homer, thus describes the first interview between Zurtosht and Gushtasp, "Learn," said Zardehusht to Gushtasp, "the rites and doctrines of the religion of excellence. For without religion there cannot be any worth in a king. When the mighty (or excellent) monarch heard him speak of the excellent religion, he accepted from him the excellent rites and doctrines." Zurtosht was at first disbelieved, and persecuted by the courtiers of Gushtasp; but having established his claim as a divine prophet, and convinced the King and his court by performing several miracles, he was taken into favour.

Gushtasp not only himself embraced the religion propounded by Zurtosht, but used all his influence to spread it among other kings and the wise men of the world. The King's premier, Furshoster, and Jamasp, the most learned men of the age, are said to have become disciples of the prophet. These two illustrious personages traversed different parts of Iran as the apostles of the Zoroastrian doctrines, and succeeded in converting all the Iranians to the new religion.

The example of the King would of course soon be followed by the nobles and the people; and the monarch having accepted the new religion, there was little difficulty in propagating it among his subjects. On learning that the King was prepared to acknowledge his claims, Zurtosht produced the sacred books called Avasta, which he had brought with him to the court of the King. These books were written in the Zend language, a language understood to have existed as far back as three or four thousand years ago.

Some European authors contend that the Zend language is derived from the Sanscrit, but this has never been satisfactorily proved. Authors of reputation are agreed in the opinion that the language in which the Parsee Scriptures are written first originated in the province of Bactria, which, in the Vandidad, is called *Bukhdi*. The Sanscrit, as is now generally believed, was first spoken in the country situated to the south of Bactria, or in the region bounding the north of Afghanistan, in the vicinity of the range of mountains known as Hindoo Koosh; hence some similarity in the two languages from the proximity of the countries in which they originated, but it has never been satisfactorily proved that the Zend was derived from the Sanscrit.

The celebrated Professor Bopp is of opinion that the Zend is a much more improved language than the Sanscrit, and is as old as the language of the Veds, which was composed three or four thousand years ago. This learned author, who has compiled a comparative grammar of several European and Asiatic classical languages on the basis of the Zend says, "that the Zend displays that independence of the Sanscrit which Rask claims for it perhaps in too high a degree," and adds that "we are unwilling to receive the Zend as a mere dialect of the Sanscrit, and to which we are compelled to ascribe an independent existence, resembling that of the Latin as compared with the Greek, or the old Northern with the Gothic. It in many respects reaches beyond, and is an improvement on the Sanscrit."

The books, produced by the Prophet and generally called Avasta, contained twenty-one noosk, or volumes. The following table shows the Zend names of these volumes, with their corresponding ones in Pehlvi:—

	ZEND.	PEHLVI.
1.	Yatha	Suttood-Yeasht.
2.	A-hoo	Suttoodgur.
3.	Verio	Vehest-Mathre.
4.	A-tha	Bug.
5.	Ratoos	Davajdeh-Hamas.
6.	Ussad	Nadoor.
7.	Chid	Pachem.
8.	Hucha	Ruttoostide.
9.	Vungéhoos	Burrus.
10.	Dujda	Kussusroob.
11.	Munungho	Vishtasp.
12.	Sicuthénanam	Khesuth.
13.	Ungéhoos	Suffund.
14.	Muzdaí	Jursut.
15.	Khusthremchai	Bugan-Teasht.
16.	A-hoorai	Neeyadoom.
17.	Aa	Hoosparem.
18.	Eem	Davasroosid.
19.	Durregobio	Ushkarum.
20.	Dadada	Vandidad.
21.	Vastarem	Hadokht.

The majority of these works are not in the possession of the Parsees of this day. They are supposed to have been destroyed either during the invasion of Persia by the Macedonian, Alexander, or immediately after the conquest of that country by the Arabs, who entertained so great a hatred for the ancient religion of Persia, that they sought out and collected all the works of Zurtosht and his disciples which they could find in Persia, and destroyed nearly the whole of them.

A few of the works above mentioned, however, survived destruction, and are now in the possession of the Parsees. They are the Vandidad, Yaçna, or Izashné, and Vispard. These three together are designated Vandidad Sade. Ogum Decha, Khurdah-Avasta, and the Yeshts and fragments of Vistasp Noosk, Hadokht Noosk, and Damdad Noosk are also to be found. The first, fourth, seventh, eighth, and ninth of these works are mostly filled with prescriptions for religious ceremonies and instructions for the practice of the Zoroastrian religion. They also contain injunctions for the adoration of the Almighty, and abound with moral precepts. The Izashné, Vispard, Khurdah-Avasta, and the Yeshts are books of prayers.

It may be mentioned here that the oldest manuscript copies now existing of the Vandidad and Izashné were deposited in the Royal Library at Copenhagen by Professor Erasmus Rask, who, in the year eighteen hundred and twenty, visited Bombay and passed through Persia. The copy of the first-named work bears date the 24th day of the fourth month of the year of Yezdezard,

692, A.D. 1323. The latter work is dated ten months later.

In India the oldest manuscript copy of the Vandidad is to be found in the library of the late Mulla Feroz, High Priest of the Kudmi sect of the Parsees. Manuscript copies of these works are also deposited in the Imperial Library, Paris; in the University Library, Oxford; and in the British, as well as the East India Company's Museum, London. Professor N. L. Westergard, of Copenhagen, published an edition of the Vandidad Sade, in the Zend character, in the year 1854. Professor Spiegel has also published the Avasta in the original Zend text, together with the original Pehlvi translation, and is said to be preparing an English version of the same for the press.

While enumerating the liturgical works of the Parsees, now extant, it may be mentioned that it has been asserted by Richardson, Kennedy, Jones, and some other European authors, but without any satisfactory proof, that the Zend books of the Parsees were fabricated by the Parsee priests upon their arrival in India in the seventh century. Other Orientalists are of opinion that they must have been written after the days of Ardeshir Babekan, who, as we have seen, restored the religion of Zoroaster in the third century. The former hypothesis is utterly gratuitous. It is altogether improbable and beyond belief that a persecuted race of men, driven from their native country, and suffering vicissitudes of no ordinary kind—refugees, indeed, flying for their lives—could have compiled such elaborate works as the Vandidad, Vispard, and Izashné.

On this point we have the opinion of a learned German author. Adelung, in his "Mithridates," says, "In the Zend some writings still exist which have been made known by Anquetil du Perron; and these, when the grounds on which their antiquity are maintained are duly considered, will be found to be the oldest works extant except those of the Hebrews and the poems of Homer." Professor Rask has also maintained that the Zend was a living language and the spoken language of Media, and that the Vandidad, as it exists, was written before the time of Alexander the Great.

Dr. Bird, in his discourse on Oriental literature, read at the anniversary meeting of the Bombay branch of the Royal Asiatic Society, in the year 1844, declares that "Professor Rask supposes, with great probability, that the Zend was the popular language, at least of a great part of Iran, and not merely a sacred dialect introduced for religious purposes. The testimony of so ancient an author as Masudi, that the books called Asta (Avasta), and its commentary, the Pazend, were in existence in his time, establishes the comparative antiquity of the Zend Avasta, and that the language of it is not a forgery of modern times."

Professor Heeren, in his elaborate historical treatise, declares that "few remains of antiquity have undergone such attentive examination as the books of the Zend Avasta. This criticism has, however, turned out to their advantage; the genuineness of the principal compositions, particularly the Vandidad and Izashné, as religious books of the ancient Persians, has been demonstrated; and we may consider as completely ascertained all that regards the rank of each book of the Zend Avasta." Another well known author, Rhode, who has examined the Zend works with scrupulous care, has come to the conclusion that the collection of books called the Zend Avasta "contains either all or most of the compositions which existed before the destruction of the Persian empire by Alexander."

Grotefend, another learned antiquarian, in his essay on the cuneiform inscriptions, thus delivers himself: "The ancient existence of the Zend dialect, first discovered by M. du Perron, being as little subject to be called in question as that of the Pehlvi or Parsee, we therefore consider the Zend Avasta as a genuine religious code of the old Persians, by reference to which we are enabled to judge of their peculiar notions in matters of religion. The conformity in point of language discoverable upon comparing the inscriptions with the manuscripts of the Zend Avasta, proves equally beyond a doubt the ancient existence of the Zend, as the Sassanide inscriptions deciphered by M. de Sacy, prove that the Pehlvi flourished some centuries later."

Abbé Foucher is also of opinion that the Zend books were composed in the reign of Gushtasp. Anthony Troyer, the learned translator of the Dabistan, says, "We may reasonably believe that the Zend books were written at a time when the Zend was a living, nay the dominant, language in those countries, where these books first appeared; that is, in Georgia, in Iran, and in Azerbejan." Sir John Malcolm and Mr. J. B.

Fraser, in their histories of Persia, both maintain the antiquity and the authenticity of the Zend Avasta.

It will thus be seen that the genuineness of the Zend Avasta cannot be impeached, the most learned and acute scholars of Europe frankly recognising the Zend as one of the most ancient of languages. The Zend Avasta itself contains intrinsic evidence of its being composed more than 2,500 years ago, viz., in the reign of Gushtasp. The Parsee Scriptures do not mention any event, king, or person after Gushtasp and Zurtosht. The Pehlvi works, compiled in the reign of Ardeshir Bubekan, all speak of the existence of the Zend Avasta. The works "Dinkard," "Vujurkard," "Shayest Nashayest," and "Nirangestan," believed to have been originally compiled by the disciples of Zurtosht, all make mention of the Zend Avasta promulgated by Zurtosht.

Mahomedan authors, again, who flourished about a thousand years ago, make mention of Zurtosht and his Zend Avasta. These evidences must of course be held sufficient to establish not only the antiquity, but also the authenticity and genuineness of the sacred writings of the Parsees, some parts of which the followers of Zoroaster have at all hazards preserved up to this day.

Besides the Zend Avasta, there are a few works in Pehlvi, Pazend, and Persian, relating to the religion of Zoroaster, but it is unnecessary to speak of them here, as in writing on the Parsee religion, it is enough to notice those books which are recognised as sacred by the professors of that religion.

Now what is the religion of the Parsees, as propounded in the sacred works above enumerated? What do we find to be the nature of the religion of Zoroaster, on examination of the Zend Avasta? The Persians, before the advent of that prophet, were, more or less, worshippers of idols. The mission of Zoroaster, therefore, was to effect a thorough reformation of the religion, or rather superstition prevalent in Persia, and to lead the people into the paths of virtue and piety.

He is said to have performed several miracles for the purpose of convincing his followers of the truth of his doctrines and revelations. The religion propounded by him is a simple form of theism, recognising but one God, the Creator, Ruler, and Preserver of the universe, without form, and invisible. To Him is assigned a place above all, and to Him every praise is to be given for all the good in this world and all the blessings we enjoy. Zoroastrianism does not require any image of God to be made for the purpose of worship, as to Him is attributed no form, shape, or colour. He is an immense light from which all glory, bounty, and goodness flow. He is represented as the mightiest, the most just, and the most benevolent. His mercies are as boundless as His being. The adoration or worship of any other object is blasphemous. Such, in short, is the picture of God as depicted in the religion of Zurtosht.

The whole foundation of the sacred or religious works of the Parsees is, as it were, built upon three important injunctions which pervade the Parsee Scriptures, and are pithily expressed by three significant terms used in the Avasta, viz., *Homuté*, *Hookhté*, and *Vurusté*, which mean purity of speech, purity of action, and purity of thought. This is the moral of the Parsee religion, and on it the whole structure of the Zend Avasta is raised.

A perusal of these works will show that they inculcate those sublime doctrines and sound precepts of morality which command the respect of every civilized nation on earth. Evil actions are placed in their proper light and condemned, whereas the practice of every virtue is enjoined, highly extolled and sanctioned by reward in this as well as in the next world. The Avasta seeks strongly to impress that virtue alone is happiness in this world; and that its path is the path of peace. It is a garment of honour, while wickedness is represented as a robe of shame. The most acceptable sacrifices to God are good actions, while intentions, as well as actions, must be good to be acceptable to Him. The best court of equity is a good conscience. Truth is laid down as the basis of all excellence; untruth is punishable as one of the worst of sins. Industry, inasmuch as it is never unfruitful, and is a guard to innocence and a bar to temptation, is highly recommended, while idleness is represented as the parent of want and shame. Principles of hospitality, general philanthropy, and benevolence, are strongly inculcated.

We now quote the opinions of unprejudiced European authors as to what Parseeism truly is. Anquetil du Perron, the celebrated Frenchman, who was the first European who examined the Zend Avasta, is an able illustrator of the Parsee faith. His extensive acquaintance with the facts of the system which he has unfolded is a sufficient guarantee for the weight to be attached to his opinions.

In his "Critical view of the theological and ceremonial system of Zurtosht," he says, "the first point in the theological system of Zoroaster is to recognise and adore the Master of all that is good, the Principle of all righteousness, Ormuzd, according to the form of worship prescribed by him, and with purity of thought, of word, and of action. A purity which is marked and preserved by purity of body, which must always accompany it, and which is found only in entire submission to the law of Zoroaster. Next, to have a respect, accompanied with gratitude, for the intelligence to which Ormuzd has committed the care of Nature,—to take in our actions their attributes for models,—to copy in our conduct the harmony which reigns in the different parts of the universe,—and generally to honour Ormuzd (the Almighty as he is styled in the Avasta) in all that he has produced.

"The second point of the religion of the Parsees consists in detesting the author of all evil, moral and physical, Ahriman—his productions, and his works; and to contribute, as far as in us lies, to exalt the glory of Ormuzd, by enfeebling the tyranny which the Evil Principle exercises over the world which the Good Principle has created.

"On these two points bear the prayers, the religious practices, the civil usages, and the moral precepts, which are presented in the Zend and Pehlvi books; and these different objects arise, as we shall see, from the theological ideas of the legislator of the Persians.

"Prayer is one of the duties most strongly enjoined, because man, continually exposed to the assaults of Ahriman, (the evil principle) stands in need of the succour which it procures; and because it affords opportunity for those intelligences to whom it is addressed, to fulfil the object for which they were created.

"The priest prays for himself, for all the Parsees, and in particular, as in the days of Herodotus, for the king whom Ormuzd has placed over his people; and to give greater efficiency to his prayers, unites them to those of all the Parsees, of all the souls acceptable to Ormuzd, which have existed, or shall exist until the resurrection. He declares also that he takes part in the good deeds of all the righteous, and that he joins his action to theirs.

This communion of prayers and actions appears in all the forms and all the offices which compose the liturgical works of the Parsees. It is well adapted to maintain the spirit of peace and union which ought to characterize a people who profess to adore the Author of all good.

"The Parsees commence prayers with a sincere confession of the sins they have committed."*

This is a pretty fair account of the theological system of Zoroaster reduced to practice. Ahriman should, however, be taken in an allegorical sense to denote the cause of the temptation under which man often falls into evil.

Dr. Hyde, in his celebrated work on the ancient Parsee religion, also says that, "The Persians, from the beginning of their existence as a nation, always believed in only one and the same true and omnipotent God. They believed in all the attributes of the Deity believed by us; and God is called in their own writings, the Doer, the Creator, the Governor and the Preserver of the world. They also believed that the Deity was eternal (without beginning or end) and omnipotent, with a

* Translated from the French by the Rev. Murray Mitchel.

great many attributes, which to enumerate particularly would be tedious. They also believed this Deity to be the judge of all men, and that there was to come a general resurrection of every man, to be judged and accounted according to his merits or demerits. And they also believed that God has prepared for the blessed a place of happiness called heaven or paradise. And as there was a heaven for the good, there was also a place of torture for the wicked (as may be proved from their old works), where they undergo a punishment for their faults and misdeeds. They acknowledged that they sinned daily, but proposed themselves to be penitent for all the sins committed by them either by thought, word, or deed."

In alluding to these remarks of Dr. Hyde, Sir William Ouseley says, "I sincerely join in respecting the old Persian worship, and sympathize in lamenting the infamous persecution which has caused its decay."

We have said above that the Zoroastrians are theists. There is no doubt of their being monotheists; they tolerate no other worship but that of the Supreme Being; and we are confirmed in this view not only by the European authorities quoted above, but by the practices and religious prayers of the Parsees at this day. That the Parsees are not idolators is sufficiently plain to all the Europeans who come in contact with this community. The images which existed in Persia when Zurtosht promulgated his doctrines and reformed the national religion were soon destroyed, and active efforts are said to have been made to extinguish heretical forms of worship, and destroy the idols worshipped in the bordering countries. Xerxes, the immediate successor of Gushtasp, had such a hatred for idolatry that he destroyed all the Grecian temples dedicated to the gods.

The charge of fire, sun, water, and air worship has, however, been brought against the Parsees by those not sufficiently acquainted with the Zoroastrian faith to form a just opinion. The Parsees themselves repel the charge with indignation. Ask a Parsee whether he is a worshipper of the sun or fire, and he will emphatically answer—No! This declaration itself, coming from one whose own religion is Zoroastrianism, ought to be sufficient to satisfy the most sceptical. God, according to Parsee faith, is the emblem of glory, refulgence, and light, and in this view, a Parsee, while engaged in prayer, is directed to stand before the fire,* or to direct his face towards the sun as the most proper symbols of the Almighty.

All Eastern historians have acknowledged that the Persians from the most early time were no idolators, but worshipped one God, the Creator of the World, under the symbol of Fire, and such is also the present practice among their descendants in India.

The following is the opinion of Dean Prideaux on this subject:—"They (the Persians) abominating all images, worshipped God only by fire. Light was the truest symbol of the good God, and therefore they always worshipped him before fire as being the cause of light, and especially before the sun, as being in their opinion the perfectest fire, and causing the perfectest light. And for this reason, in all their temples, they had fire continually burning on altars erected in them for that purpose, and before these sacred fires they offered up

* In Bombay at present there are three Fire-temples for public worship. The first of these was erected in the 1153 year of Yezdeziyd, 1780 of the Christian era, by a wealthy Parsee named Dadysett. The second was built about the year 1830, at the expense of the late Hormusjee Bomonjee, Esq.; and the third one was erected by the late Framjee Cowasjee, Esq., in the year 1844, at a cost of Rs. 250,000, or £25,000.

all their public devotions, as likewise they did all their private devotions before their private fires in their own houses. Thus did they pay the highest honour to light, as being in their opinion the truest representative of the Good God, but always hated darkness as being what they thought the truest representative of the Evil God, whom they ever had in the utmost detestation, as we now have the Devil." Sir William Ouseley perfectly agrees with Dean Prideaux, and says—"I shall here express my firm belief that the first Persian altars blazed in honour of God alone; as likewise, that the present disciples of Zurtosht, both in India and the mother country, Iran or Persia, have no other object when they render to fire a semblance of veneration." Dr. Hyde, an English theologian, whom we have already quoted, does not hesitate to declare that the ancient Medes and Persians were worshippers of the true God, a race of the faithful, and haters of idolatry.

Anquetil du Perron, than whom no other European has more critically examined the Zend Avasta, says that "the religion prevalent in Persia till the destruction of the empire, and carried into India by the Parsees, who still possess it, merits more attention than almost any other. It was at first pure theism, though even in the time of Abraham debased by heterodox opinions; but they have ever zealously preserved the doctrine of the unity of God; and we are not to conclude from the veneration they showed, and still show, to fire and the sun, that they have ever adored either the element or the luminary. Zoroaster, their great teacher, directed them to turn towards the sun or the fire when they prayed; but the prayers which they recite in this position are addressed solely to the Sovereign Being, and not to the symbols of Him.

"The doctrines, however, which these miracles" (*i.e.* those of Zoroaster) "confirmed, were wise and rational. They taught the unity of God; His omnipotence; His goodness towards men; a great veneration for fire, the visible type of the invisible divinity; and a great aversion for Ahriman, the evil principle, the instigator of evil thoughts, but not co-eternal with God. The morality contained in the books of Zoroaster is very pure, and all founded on the love of our neighbour."

The following extract from Forbes' "Oriental Memoirs," also proves that the Parsees are not worshippers of the elements.

"These fires (*i. e.* the sacred fires of the

Parsees) are attended day and night by the Andiaroos or priests, and are never permitted to expire. They are preserved in a large ehafing-dish, earefully supplied with fuel, perfumed by a small quantity of sandal-wood or other aromaties. The vulgar and illiterate worship this saered flame, as also the sun, moon, and stars, without regard to the invisible Creator; but the learned and judicious adore only the Almighty Fountain of Light, the author and disposer of all things, under the symbol of fire. Zoroaster and the ancient magi, whose memories they revere, and whose works they are said to preserve, never taught them to consider the sun as anything more than a ereature of the great Creator of the universe: they were to revere it as His best and fairest image, and for the numberless blessings it diffuses on the earth. The sacred flame was intended only as a perpetual monitor to preserve their purity, of whieh this element is so expressive a symbol. But superstition and fable have, through a lapse of ages, corrupted the stream of the religious system whieh in its souree was pure and sublime."

The following extraet from Hanway's Travels is one of the numerous evidenees that the

Parsees are monotheists:—"He (Zoroaster, the founderof the ancient religion of the Persians) considered light as the most perfect symbol of true wisdom and intellectual endowment; and darkness the representative of things hurtful and destructive. From hence he was led to inculcate an abhorrence of all images, and to teach his followers to worship God only, under the form of fire, considering the brightness, activity, purity, and incorruptibility of that element, as bearing the most perfect resemblance to the nature and perfections of the good deity. For the same reason the Persians showed a particular veneration to the sun, which was founded on their belief that it is the noblest creature of the visible world. . .

"He taught that there is one supreme, independent, and self-existent being."

Sir John Malcolm in his splendid work on the history of Persia, acknowledges that the reproachful name of fire-worshippers is not merited by the Parsees. He says—"God, he" (Zoroaster) "taught, existed from all eternity, and was like infinity of time and space. There were, he averred, two principles in the universe—good and evil. Light was the type of good, darkness, of the evil spirit; and God had said unto Zoroaster, 'My light is concealed under all that shines.' Hence the disciple of that prophet, when he prays in a temple, turns towards the sacred fire that burns upon its altar; and when in the open air towards the sun, as the noblest of all lights, and that by which God sheds His Divine influences over the whole earth, and perpetuates the works of His creation. . . . His religion inculcated the worship of one immortal and beneficent Creator. Whatever might have been his (Zoroaster's) intention, his introduction of flame from an earthly substance, as the symbol of God, opened a wide door for superstition. There can be no doubt that the devotion intended for the Deity by Zoroaster has been given to the symbol by many of his followers, who have merited by such a practice the reproachful name of worshippers of fire."

Captain J. A. Pope, who has studied the Parsee religion, and has deliberately expressed his opinion on the morality of that faith, thus writes:—"They" (the Parsees) "follow as near as possible the tenets of Zurtusht, professing their belief in one God, considering fire only as an emblem of his purity, and the sun as the most perfect of his work; they believe also in the rewards and punishments in a future state, as related in the revelations of Ardai Viraf."

The following is an extract from Niebuhr's travels through Arabia and other countries in the East. "The Parsees, followers of Zerdust, or Zoroaster, adore one God only, Eternal and Almighty. They pay, however, a certain worship to the sun, the moon, the stars, and to fire, as visible images of the invisible Divinity. Their veneration for the element of fire induces them to keep a sacred fire constantly burning, which they feed with odoriferous wood, both in the temples and in the houses of private persons who are in easy circumstances."

The Rev. J. Ovington, who visited Surat in the year 1689, says, from personal observation, that "the Parsees own and adore one Supreme Being, to whom, as he is the original of all things, they dedicate the first day of every month in a solemn observance of his worship. And enjoin, besides these, some others for the celebration of public prayer."

The following extract from Butler's "Horæ Biblicæ" also explains the nature of the Parsee faith:—"Fire was considered by Zoroaster as the purest symbol of the Divinity, and the original element from which Ormuzd produced all beings: he therefore enjoined his disciples to keep up a perpetual fire, and to perform other devotional exercises in the presence of fire; and every supposed corruption of fire is forbidden, under the severest penalties. To every act of devotion purity of heart is necessary; and to purity of heart Zoroaster supposes purity of body greatly contributes."

The following is from "Rollin's Ancient History":—"As the Magi held images in utter abhorrence, they worshipped God only under the form of fire, looking upon that, on account of its purity, brightness, activity, subtilty, fecundity, and incorruptibility, as the most perfect symbol of the Deity."

The subjoined extract from the *Asiatic Journal* for April, 1840, also explains the reasons of the observances paid to fire:

"The observances paid to fire (it is unjust to call them worship) are only parts of a ritual which prescribes a similar respect for, and mention in prayers of, all the classes of animated nature, and some objects inanimate. The respect paid to fire is more prominent than the other parts of the ritual, inasmuch as that element is considered the terrestrial image of the Supreme Being."

Mrs. Postans, a very intelligent lady, who

visited Bombay about fifteen years ago, and who made herself acquainted with the manners and customs of the Parsees, says, in a work recently published by her:—"I have used this title (fire-worshippers) in conformity with the popular English notion of Parsee worship; but the term is, I believe, quite unfounded. They do not worship either the elements or the heavenly bodies, being, in fact, pure Deists, and regarding the works of God's hand as to be reverenced only as proofs of the Divine power." Various Mahomedan authors have likewise freed the Parsees from the charge of the worship of the elements. The authors of the "Tarikh-i-Tabri," "Shah-Namah," and "Dabestan" take the same view of Parsee worship as the European authors above quoted.

That the whole of the Zend Avasta, the sacred work of the Parsees, abounds with high moral precepts does not admit of a doubt, and that it impresses upon the minds of its believers the principles of moral duty is evident from the customs, mode of living, and characters of the Parsees. With religion Zurtosht has combined moral philosophy in a remarkable degree; and it was in this very spirit that his system was attempted to be revived in the reign of Ardeshir Babekan. That monarch assembled all the learned men and priests of the Empire to deliberate upon and devise the best plan for restoring the ancient purity of the national religion, which had been neglected and forgotten since the days of Alexander.

A monster meeting composed of more than 40,000 men invited from all parts of the kingdom is said to have been held by that king, of whom the most able were selected, and under the guidance of the pious and learned Ardai Veraf, a code of morals called the "Revelations of Ardai Veraf" was composed and published for the people. This celebrated work was dictated by Ardai Veraf. It professes to be a description of what he beheld in a vision in which he was transported into the other world, and visited the abodes of the deceased, that inherited heaven or hell, according to their acts while they sojourned upon earth.

Many Parsees believe in the reality of the narrative, and regard the revelations as genuine, whilst others, holding a more philosophic view, look upon the work as simply a vivid imaginative picture of the future destiny of men who follow the good or bad examples described in the revelations. They believe the work was composed for the vulgar with the object of encouraging virtue and morality, and deterring them from immoral conduct and pursuits. The proposed object of the revelations, was one greatly to be desired, namely, to banish heresy and schism from the earth, and to restore the worship of the true God to its wonted purity. The national religion of Persia, from the invasion of Alexander to the accession of Ardeshir Babekan, had become much corrupted, and these revelations effected a reform.

Regarded in this light, the Ardai Veraf Namah is an excellent work, the whole tenor of it being strictly moral, while no one can read it without being impressed with an idea of the greatness and goodness of God, and imbued with sound principles of morality. Capt. J. A. Pope has translated the work into English, and on publishing it in the year 1816, declared that the motives which led him to undertake its publication, "arose from a strong desire to be more intimately acquainted with the principles of a morality he admired, and of the daily exercise of benevolence that sprang from those principles." He further trusts, that "it will be the means of removing many an ill-founded opinion with regard to the morality of this interesting tribe." Zoroaster has said, and the Zend Avasta proclaims in every page, that men are saved only by their good deeds in this world; every soul is punished or rewarded according to his conduct, and the motives by which he was actuated in his mundane career. Nothing can be more true, nothing more compatible with the nicest sense of justice—rewards according to merit, punishment according to crime. And these, in fact, are the very objects which the revelations of Ardai Veraf profess to show and prove. The description which the Parsee sage gives of heaven and hell, the happy state in which the good and virtuous souls were located, and the torments and miseries which those who had walked in evil ways were condemned to suffer, are eminently calculated to stimulate virtuous conduct, and induce the evil to amend his ways, and lead a life of piety and holiness.

Ardai Veraf speaks of a place that he beheld, which seemed to him to be composed of diamonds and rubies, the splendour of which surpassed that of the sun at noonday, and bore resemblance to flashes of vivid lightning. That it appeared like a spacious garden, planted with trees and shrubs of various kinds, and adorned with rivulets and springs. That the trees were alive with singing-birds, filling the air with their melodious notes. That the spring sent out the scent of roses. That this was the residence of those who had worshipped none other than one God, and had walked in the way of holiness and devotion all their lives, performing the duties enjoined by the laws of God with zeal and activity; that the gems represented their virtues, while their souls were absorbed in splendours which could not be gazed upon. On the other hand the place of the sinner, the evil disposed, and the wicked, is described in the darkest colours imaginable. When it is remembered that this picturesque style of writing appeals forcibly to an Eastern mind, it cannot be doubted that it held forth the most powerful inducements to the practice of virtue, and the shunning of evil.

What the nature of the religion, revived in the reign of Ardashir Babekan, and up to this day professed by the Parsees of India is, will be best explained by the following injunctions given to Ardai Veraf, when he is said to have returned from his mission for the instruction of the people in the way of righteousness.

"Listen, O Ardai Veraf!" said the Angel,

"without trouble nothing can be attained, the poor day labourer is worthy of his hire, and thus those who perform good actions will have their reward in eternal life according to their several merits. The life of man is of short duration, and many troubles and anxieties fall to his lot; and a man after fifty years of prosperity and happiness, may be, by some unforeseen accident, reduced to sickness and poverty.

"Many are tried by this criterion, and but few are found worthy. To suffer a day of pain, after fifty years of pleasure, is too much for them, and they complain, in bitterness of spirit, to the Creator of all good, of His injustice and cruelty, without remembering the good they have so long enjoyed, or calling to mind the eternity of punishment in reserve for the wicked. Therefore, O Ardai Veraf! walk yourself in the paths of righteousness, and teach others also to do so. Recollect that your body will return to dust, but that your soul, if rich in good works, will mount to immortality, and partake of the happiness you have already witnessed.

"Take less care of your body, and more of your soul; the pains and aches of the body are easily cured, but who can minister to the diseases of the soul? When you set out on a journey in the lower world you provide yourselves, and take with you money, clothes, provisions, and are prepared against all the exigencies of the road, but what do you provide yourselves with for your last journey of the soul from the lower to the upper world; and whose friendship have you to assist you on the way? Hear, O Ardai Viraf! and I will describe to you the provisions requisite for the voyage to eternal life.

"In the first place, the friend who will assist you is God; but to attain his friendship you must walk in his ways, and place in him the firmest reliance. The provisions must be faith and hope, and the remembrance of your good works. Thy body, O, Ardai Viraf! may be likened unto a horse, and thy soul to its rider, and the provisions requisite for the support of both are good actions. But as with a feeble rider the horse is ill managed, so with a feeble horse the rider is but ill accommodated, care ought to be taken that both are kept in order; so in a spiritual sense, the soul and body must be kept in order by a succession of good actions. Even in the world the multitude would sneer at a man who took more care of his horse than of himself; for this reason a man ought to take more care of his soul than of his body. God! O Ardai Viraf! requires only two things of the sons of men; the first, that they should not sin; the second, that they should be grateful for the many blessings He is continually bestowing on them.

"Let the world, O Ardai Viraf! be taught not to set their hearts on the pleasures and vanities of life, as nothing can be carried away with them. You have already seen the rewards given to the good and deserving; how they have been repaid for all their trouble; the poor and the rich, the king and the peasant, here receive honours and distinction, according to their good works. The herdsman and shepherd, you have seen their condition.

"In youth, and in the prime of manhood, when blessed with health and vigour, you suppose that your strength will never fail; that your riches, your lands, your houses, and your honours, will remain for ever; that your gardens will be always green, and your vineyards fruitful; but O Ardai Viraf! teach them not to think so; teach them the danger of such a way of thinking—all, all will pass away as a dream.

"The flowers fade, and give lessons unto man that he is unwilling to profit by. Yea, the world itself will pass away, and nothing will remain but God."

It is unnecessary to defend the morality or excellence of such sentiments as these; but many causes have operated to place the religion of the Parsees in a false light. A persecuted race, destitute of many of its sacred books, and coming in contact with a people highly jealous of their own religion, and to whom the slightest touch from one of another caste was a source of impurity, it was natural that the Parsees should have contracted, as time passed on, many of the practices of their neighbours.

The first Parsees in India had of necessity to follow certain of the Hindoo practices, in order to secure the protection, assistance, and good-will of the Hindoo princes, in whose country they took refuge. Time rolled on, and succeeding generations of Parsees fell into the error that these borrowed practices were sanctioned by their own religion. "Our forefathers did so," and, according to Asiatic ideas, the children thought that their ancestors could do no wrong. The study of the few religious books which they had with them was not cultivated, for there were few learned men among the body. The result was that many of the usages, customs, practices, and prejudices of the Hindoos were received and acted upon by the Parsees. It is thus that we may easily explain how it is that an ignorant Parsee, or his wife, at the present day, sends an offering of a cocoa-nut to the *Holi*, or a cup of oil to the *Hunoo-man*, or cakes, sugar, and flowers to the sea.

The Parsee punchayet, some twenty-five years ago, took steps with the view of eradicating such ceremonies and practices as had crept into their religion since their expatriation from Persia; but they did not succeed, to the extent of their wishes, with the majority of the people. Religious usages which the Parsees of India had observed for nearly twelve centuries could not easily be eradicated.

What the punchayet failed to do by compulsory measures is now sought to be done by an appeal to the sense of the people. An association composed of many influential and wealthy Parsees, and a number of young and educated men of the race, was formed in the year 1852, under the title of the "Rahnumaí Mazdiasna," or Religious Reform Association, which has for its object the regeneration of the social condition of the Parsees, and the restoration of the Zoroastrian religion to its pristine purity.

In the face of considerable opposition from the ignorant classes of the community, this association has done much good and wrought considerable changes in the social condition of the Parsees. Essays, composed in language eloquent and impressive, showing the disadvantages resulting from adhering to practices and usages which really do not belong to the religion, are read in public meetings before a crowd of eager listeners. Pamphlets by thousands have been circulated among the people, and judging from present appearances, the efforts of this body seem to have had a beneficial influence on the minds of the people.

The committee of the Sir Jamsetjee Jeejeebhoy Translation Fund, lately contributed its quota to this much-desired object. An essay on the "Origin and History of the Zend Avasta, with an account of the investigations of European authors regarding the Zend books, with suggestions for enhancing religious education among the Parsees, and particularly among the priests," was invited, and a prize of Rs. 500, or 50*l.*, offered to the successful competitor.

There were three candidates for the prize, and the essay by Mr. Sorabjee Shapoorjee, formerly Secretary of the Religious Reform Association above-mentioned, was honoured with success. It is said that this *brochure* is distinguished by considerable research, and is remarkable for the ability with which the subject is treated. Mr. Sorabjee's name is well-known in the Parsee community as the coadjutor of the indefatigable Nourosjee Fuzdoonjee in his labours for the improvement of the social and religious condition of the Parsees.

The condition of the Parsee priesthood demands improvement. Very few of them understand their liturgical works, although able to recite parrot-like all the chapters requiring to be repeated on occasions of religious ceremonies; for which services they receive the regulated fees, and from them mainly they derive a subsistence. The priesthood is an hereditary profession among the Parsees. The priest does not acquire his position from sacerdotal fitness or superior learning. Strictly speaking he cannot be called a spiritual guide. The son of a priest is also a priest, unless he chooses to follow another profession, which is not prohibited to him. But a layman cannot be a priest.

The Parsee religion does not, however, sanction this hereditary office; which is, indeed, contrary to the ancient law. The custom is merely derived from usage. Ignorant and unlearned as these priests are, they do not and cannot command the respect of the laity. The latter are more enlightened and educated than the former, and hence the position of the so-called spiritual guides has fallen into contempt. The consequence is that some of the priests have of late years given up a profession which has ceased to be honourable, and have betaken themselves to useful and industrious occupations, whilst a few have become contractors for constructing railroads in the Bombay Presidency.

It is, however, very gratifying to notice an attempt that is now being made to impart a healthy stimulus to the priesthood for the study of their religious books. In memory of the late lamented high priest of the Kudmi sect of the Parsees, an institution, styled the "Mulla Firoz Mudrissa," has been established, under the superintendence of competent teachers. Here the study of Zend, Pehlvi, and Persian, is cultivated, and many of the sons of the present ignorant priests, it is confidently hoped, will occupy a higher position in the society of their countrymen than their parents now enjoy.

Inquiring and intelligent youths from among the laity, are also now engaged in the study of their religious books; and considering the present state of Parsee society, it is probable that through their instrumentality more good will be effected than from the exertions of the priesthood. A Nourosjee Furdoonjee, a Dhunjeebhoy Framjee, or a Sorabjee Shapoorjee, can more satisfactorily propound and explain their religion than an assembly of modern priests.

The present dastoors or bishops, among the Parsees, namely Dastoor Peshotun, the successor of the learned and well-known Edul Daroo, and Mulla Ardashír, the successor of the equally renowned Mulla Feroz, are intelligent and well-informed men, possessing a considerable knowledge of their religion; but the mass of the priesthood are profoundly ignorant of its first principles. As the minds of the Parsee people are now awakening to the disgraceful state of existing matters, and as active measures are being devised for improvement, the darkness and gloom of the present will doubtless be succeeded by a bright dawn in the future.

CHAPTER VIII.

CONCLUSION.

Progress of the Parsees—Influence on the other natives of India—Home influences—Commercial prospects—Loyalty—The future of the Parsees.

In the foregoing pages, we have endeavoured to trace the progress of the small remnant of the followers of Zoroaster, who have, under the most changing vicissitudes, clung to the faith of their forefathers. We have watched this people, driven by persecution from their native land, now taking refuge in mountain fastnesses, and now wandering to the shores of the stranger to seek an asylum. At times falling a prey to the sword of an enemy, and again driven almost to desperation by the iron hand of despotism; but under all the miseries through which they have had to pass, it is curious to note the tenacity with which they have preserved those good qualities, and those distinguishing characteristics, which in ancient times rendered the Persians the foremost nation on the earth. The spirit of independence, the high courage, the truthfulness, and the energy and enterprise which distinguished their forefathers, have been preserved by the modern Parsees; and from being simply a band of fugitives on a foreign shore, they have grown into an important people, occupying an honourable and distinguished position in the Eastern empire of Great Britain.

Of all the nations now in India, the Parsees the most nearly approximate to Europeans. As we have already shown, no sooner did the Parsees come into contact with the English, and receive the privileges that belong to a British subject, than their enterprise and energy, which had so long lain dormant, awakened with renewed vitality and force. Under the fostering protection of an enlightened Government, the civilization of the Parsees commenced, and has since proceeded with such rapid strides, that year by year they are becoming more Europeanized,*

* As confirmatory of this view, we have most opportunely discovered in the *Homeward Mail* of the 19th July, 1858, the following notice of the intention of Sir Jamsetjee Jeejeebhoy to adopt the European plan of settling the entail of the baronetcy :—

" 'Our Parsee Baronet.'—We understand that Sir Jamsetjee Jeejeebhoy has invested twenty-five lakhs of rupees in the Four per Cents. for the due maintenance of the title which not only in their manners and customs, but in their thoughts and feelings. This great advance, which is not only manifested in increased commercial enterprise and aptitude for business, but is also extending to the development of intellectual tastes and pursuits, is fraught with the brightest promises for the future; and in time to come it will be found that the Parsees form the great connecting link between the English Government in India and its native subjects. Already have they exerted some influence in this direction; and when it is seen that the enlightenment, energy, and enterprise of the Parsees insure for that race a respect and esteem from the governing powers far superior to that which can be secured by the mere display of Oriental magnificence and barbaric profusion of wealth, the other natives of India must inevitably seek to follow so bright an example. That this happy state of things can only be the

has become hereditary in his family. The interest of this sum, amounting to 'ten thousand a year,' is entailed upon the future successors of the baronetcy, who will be required to assume the patronymic of its founder. The mansion at Mazagon is in like manner entailed, and Western India will, we trust, never be without a Sir Jamsetjee Jeejeebhoy, inheriting alike the virtues and the fortune of the good old man still with us, who has won the approbation of his country and the favour of her Majesty the Queen."

work of time is an undoubted fact, but we believe that eventually this influence of the Parsees will accomplish a great revolution, and secure for the British Government in India a loyalty of feeling from the other natives, such as is now accorded to it by the Parsees.

Whatever progress the Parsees have made, they have still much to do; but they have few prejudices to stand in the way of their advancement. They are neither trammelled by the miserable institution of caste, nor does their religion lie like a stumbling block to arrest their onward progress. Education, both of males and females, is now spreading; if not with gigantic strides, it is certainly advancing with sure steps, and is based upon a solid foundation. Day by day they are freeing themselves from the restraints which Oriental ignorance has imposed upon them. In their domestic relations, they are almost European; women with them are something more than the degraded playthings which they are with other Eastern nations. A Parsee's house is now becoming that which all Englishmen so greatly prize, his "home;" in which he seeks from family intercourse that solace from the cares of life, which is only to be obtained in the bosom of those who are nearest and dearest to us. The Parsee's wife is his companion, and his children are his friends. The beneficial influences of this intercourse cannot be overrated; whenever we find woman occupying a position in which she ministers to something higher than the passions of men, it is certain that that nation is on the road to civilization. In commerce, we hope we have shown that the Parsees are following close on the heels of the British; they have exhibited a comprehensiveness in their business transactions which secures for them the recognition of the commercial world as thorough men of business, while their honour and liberality gain for them the proud designation of "honest merchants."

We have already adverted to the loyalty of the Parsees, but the writer may be pardoned for once more pointing out the unshaken faith they have displayed to the British Government throughout the late disastrous rebellion in India. This has arisen not only from an innate love of order and respect for the ruling power, but from the fact that the Parsees, we may say, *thoroughly* comprehend the nature of the British Government. They truly appreciate the blessings of an enlightened rule, which instead of repressing the energies of the people, fosters their attempts at advancement, and endeavours by example to induce them to join the march of progress, and while respecting the religion and customs of the natives seeks to inspire them with a desire to rise in the scale of civilization.

Taking all these facts into consideration, we feel we are justified in claiming a bright future for the Parsees of Western India. Their progress has not resulted from the application of any artificial stimulants, but has proceeded from a deep-rooted conviction that it is in the nature of man to advance. Looking round upon the other natives of their land of adoption, the Parsees found them steeped in ignorance, remaining stationary whilst the Western world was rapidly advancing; settling in fact into an effete state which was rotting at the core. While under native rule, it is not to be wondered at that the Parsees could do no more than keep just in advance of those who were their rulers; but it is a matter of surprise that they should, under these circumstances, have preserved inviolate those precious seeds of good which they had received as a legacy from their forefathers. Those seeds, though buried in a parched ground, were not destroyed; and no sooner did the fertilizing stream of civilization fall upon them, than they germinated, took deep root, and sprang into a flourishing existence. Under British rule, the Parsees found employment for their talents; no longer repressed and kept down by the ignorance of those in authority over them, they are enabled to give full scope to their powers, and a new field has opened to them, in which they are encouraged to labour, and from which they can reap both profit and honour. The Parsees of to-day are a different race from the Parsees of twenty years ago, and we think we may safely predict that the Parsees of twenty years hence will stand far higher in the scale of civilization than even those of our own time.

Our task is now accomplished, and if the present work has succeeded in familiarizing Europeans with a race who are seeking to become, in one sense, Europeans themselves, the aim and end of the writer will have been realized.

THE END.

NEW WORKS ON INDIAN AFFAIRS.

The British Raj contrasted with its Predecessors: and an Inquiry into the Disastrous Results of the Rebellion in the North-West Provinces upon the Hopes of the People of India By DOSABHOY FRAMJEE, Manager of the *Bombay Times.*

Personal Adventures during the Indian Rebellion, in Rohilcund, Futtehghur, and Oude. By W. EDWARDS, Esq., B.C.S., Judge of Benares, and late Magistrate and Collector of Budaon, in Rohilcund. Post 8vo, price 6*s*. cloth.

The Chaplain's Narrative of the Siege of Delhi. By the Rev. J. E. W. ROTTON, Chaplain to the Forces. Post 8vo. With a Plan of the City and Siege Works. Price 10*s*. 6*d*. cloth.

The Crisis in the Punjab, from the 10th of May until the Fall of Delhi. By FREDERIC COOPER, Esq., C.S. Post 8vo, price 7*s*. 6*d*. cloth.

Eight Months' Campaign against the Bengal Sepoys during the Mutiny, 1857. By GEORGE BOURCHIER, Captain Bengal Horse Artillery. With Plans. Post 8vo, price 7*s*. 6*d*. cloth.

The Defence of Lucknow: A Diary recording the Daily Events of the Siege from 31st May to 25th September, 1857. By Captain THOMAS F. WILSON, 13th Bengal N. I., Assistant Adjutant-General. Sixth Thousand. Small post 8vo, with Plan of the Residency. Price Half-a-Crown.

Life and Correspondence of Lord Metcalfe. By JOHN WILLIAM KAYE. New and Cheap Edition, in 2 vols, small post 8vo. With Portrait. Price 12*s*. cloth.

Christianity in India. By JOHN WILLIAM KAYE, Author of "Life of Lord Metcalfe," &c. 8vo. (*In the press.*)

Narrative of the Mission from the Governor-General of India to the Court of Ava, in 1855. With Notices of the Country, Government, and People. By Captain HENRY YULE, Bengal Engineers Imperial 8vo, with 24 plates (12 coloured), 50 Woodcuts, and 4 Maps. Elegantly bound in cloth, with gilt edges, price 2*l*. 12*s*. 6*d*.

Indian Scenes and Characters, Sketched from Life. BY Prince ALEXIS SOLTYKOFF. Sixteen Plates in Tinted Lithography, with Descriptions. Colombier Folio. (*Nearly ready.*)

Suggestions towards the Future Government of India. By HARRIET MARTINEAU. Second Edition. Demy 8vo, price 5*s*. cloth.

British Rule in India: an Historical Sketch. By HARRIET MARTINEAU. Post 8vo, 2*s*. 6*d*. cloth.

Views and Opinions of Brigadier-General Jacob, C.B. Collected and Edited by Captain LEWIS PELLY, late Political Secretary Persian Expeditionary Force. Demy 8vo, price 12*s*. cloth.

The Commerce of India. By B. A. IRVING, Esq., Author of "The Theory and Practice of Caste." Post 8vo, price 7*s*. 6*d*. cloth.

Traits and Stories of Anglo-Indian Life. By Lieut.-Colonel ADDISON. With Eight Illustrations. Small Post 8vo, price 5*s*. cloth.

Tiger Shooting in India. By Lieutenant WILLIAM RICE, 25th Bombay N. I. Super-royal 8vo, with Twelve Plates in Chromo-lithography. 21*s*. cloth.

NEW PUBLICATIONS.

The Chaplain's Narrative of the Siege of Delhi. By the Rev. J. E. W. ROTTON, Chaplain to the Delhi Field Force.

Post 8vo, with a Plan of the City and Siege Works.

(Now Ready.)

The Defence of Lucknow: A STAFF-OFFICER'S DIARY. By Capt. THOS. F. WILSON, 13th Bengal N. I., Assistant-Adjutant-General.

Sixth Thousand. With Plan of the Residency. Small post 8vo., price 2s. 6d.

"This diary is intrinsically valuable."—*Leader.*

"The 'Staff Officer' supplies exact military information with distinctness."—*Globe.*

"The story of the glorious garrison of Lucknow is told in this volume with all its thrilling and painful details."—*Nonconformist.*

"It has a special interest."—*Examiner.*

Life and Correspondence of Lord Metcalfe. By JOHN WILLIAM KAYE.

New and Cheap Edition, in 2 Vols., Small Post 8vo, with Portrait, price 12s. cloth.

"One of the most valuable biographies of the present day."—*Economist.*

"An edition revised with care and judgment."—*Gobe.*

"A new and revised edition of the life of one of the greatest and purest men that ever aided in governing in India."—*Critic.*

Narrative of the Mission from the Governor-General of India to the Court of Ava in 1855. With Notices of the Country, Government, and People. By CAPTAIN HENRY YULE, Bengal Engineers.

Imperial 8vo., with 24 Plates (12 coloured), 50 Woodcuts, and 4 Maps. Elegantly bound in cloth, with gilt edges, price 2*l.* 12*s.* 6*d.*

"A stately volume in gorgeous golden covers. Such a book is in our times a rarity. Large, massive, and beautiful in itself, it is illustrated by a sprinkling of elegant wood-cuts, and by a series of admirable tinted lithographs. . . Captain Yule secures at once an eager reception of his story. We have read it with curiosity and gratification, as a fresh, full, and luminous report upon the condition of one of the most interesting divisions of Asia beyond the Ganges."—*Athenæum.*

The Education of the Human Race. Now first Translated from the German of LESSING.

Fcap. 8vo, antique cloth, price 4s.

*** This remarkable work is now first published in English.

Suggestions Towards the Future Government of India. By HARRIET MARTINEAU.

Second Edition. Demy 8vo, price 5s. cloth.

"The genuine, honest utterances of a clear, sound understanding, neither obscured nor enfeebled by party prejudice or personal selfishness."—*Daily News.*

"As the work of an honest able writer, these Suggestions are well worthy of attention, and no doubt they will generally be duly appreciated."—*Observer.*

NEW PUBLICATIONS—*continued.*

Traits and Stories of Anglo-Indian Life.

By Lieut.-Colonel Addison.

With Eight Illustrations. *(Now Ready.)*

The Autobiography of Lutfullah, a Mohamedan Gentleman, with an Account of his Visit to England.

Edited by E. B. Eastwick, Esq.

Third Edition, Small Post 8vo. Price 5s. cloth.

"We have read this book with wonder and delight. Memoirs of a live Moslem gentleman are a novelty in our letters. . . . . Lutfullah's story will aid, in its degree, to some sort of understanding of the Indian insurrection."—*Athenæum.*

"Read fifty volumes of travel, and a thousand imitations of the oriental novel, and you will not get the flavour of Eastern life and thought, or the zest of its romance, so perfectly as in Lutfullah's book. It is readable, instructive, and entertaining."—*Leader.*

"As an autobiography the book is very curious. It bears the strongest resemblance to *Gil Blas* of anything we have ever read."—*Spectator.*

"Everyone who is interested in the present state of matters in India should read Lutfullah's own account of himself and his people, as well as their peculiar and general feeling towards the Feringees."—*Globe.*

"A treasure as well as a rarity in literature." *Eclectic Review.*

The Life and Correspondence of Sir John Malcolm, G.C.B. By John William Kaye.

Two Volumes, 8vo. With Portrait. Price 36s. cloth.

"The biography is replete with interest and information, deserving to be perused by the student of Indian history, and sure to recommend itself to the general reader."—*Athenæum.*

"One of the most interesting of the recent biographies of our great Indian statesmen."—*National Review.*

"This book deserves to participate in the popularity which it was the good fortune of Sir John Malcolm to enjoy."—*Edinburgh Review.*

"Mr. Kaye has used his materials well, and has written an interesting narrative, copiously illustrated with valuable documents."—*Examiner.*

British Rule in India. By Harriet Martineau.

Fifth Thousand. Price 2s. 6d. cloth.

"A good compendium of a great subject."—*National Review.*

"A succinct and comprehensive volume."—*Leader.*

Tiger Shooting in India.

By Lieutenant William Rice, 25th Bombay N. I.

Super Royal 8vo. With Twelve Plates in Chroma-lithography. 21s. cloth.

"These adventures, told in handsome large print, with spirited chromo-lithographs to illustrate them, make the volume before us as pleasant reading as any record of sporting achievements we have ever taken in hand."—*Athenæum.*

"A remarkably pleasant book of adventures during several seasons of 'large game' hunting in Rajpootana. The twelve chromolithographs are very valuable accessories to the narrative; they have wonderful spirit and freshness."—*Globe.*

"A good volume of wild sport, abounding in adventure, and handsomely illustrated with coloured plates from spirited designs by the author."—*Examiner.*

MR. RUSKIN'S WORKS ON ART.

Notes on the Pictures in the Exhibition of the Royal Academy, &c., for 1858. By JOHN RUSKIN.

Fifth Thousand. 8vo, *price One Shilling.*

The Political Economy of Art. Price 2s. 6d. cloth.

"A most able, eloquent, and well-timed work. We hail it with satisfaction, thinking it calculated to do much practical good, and we cordially recommend it to our readers."—*Witness.*

"Mr. Ruskin's chief purpose is to treat the artist's power, and the art itself, as items of the world's wealth, and to show how these may be best evolved, produced, accumulated, and distributed."—*Athenæum.*

"We never quit Mr. Ruskin without being the better for what he has told us, and we therefore recommend this little volume, like all his other works, to the perusal of our readers."—*Economist.*

"This book, daring, as it is, glances keenly at principles, of which some are among the articles of ancient codes, while others are evolving slowly to the light."—*Leader.*

The Elements of Drawing.

Second Edition. Crown 8vo. *With Illustrations drawn by the Author. Price* 7s. 6d., *cloth.*

"The rules are clearly and fully laid down; and the earlier exercises always conducive to the end by simple and unembarrassing means. The whole volume is full of liveliness."—*Spectator.*

"We close this book with a feeling that, though nothing supersedes a master, yet that no student of art should launch forth without this work as a compass."—*Athenæum.*

"It will be found not only an invaluable acquisition to the student, but agreeable and instructive reading for any one who wishes to refine his perceptions of natural scenery, and of its worthiest artistic representations."—*Economist.*

"Original as this treatise, is it cannot fail to be at once instructive and suggestive."—*Literary Gazette.*

"The most useful and practical book on the subject which has ever come under our notice."—*Press.*

Modern Painters, Vol. IV. On Mountain Beauty.

Imperial 8vo, *with Thirty-five Illustrations engraved on Steel, and* 116 *Woodcuts, drawn by the Author. Price* 2l. 10s. *cloth.*

"Considered as an illustrated volume, this is the most remarkable which Mr. Ruskin has yet issued. The plates and woodcuts are profuse, and include numerous drawings of mountain form by the author, which prove Mr. Ruskin to be essentially an artist. He is an unique man, both among artists and writers."—*Spectator.*

"The present volume of Mr. Ruskin's elaborate work treats chiefly of mountain scenery, and discusses at length the principles involved in the pleasure we derive from mountains and their pictorial representation. The singular beauty of his style, the hearty sympathy with all forms of natural loveliness, the profusion of his illustrations form irresistible attractions."—*Daily News.*

Modern Painters, Vol. III. Of Many Things.

With Eighteen Illustrations drawn by the Author, and engraved on Steel. Price 38s. *cloth.*

"Every one who cares about nature, or poetry, or the story of human development—every one who has a tinge of literature or philosophy, will find something that is for him in this volume."—*Westminster Review.*

"Mr. Ruskin is in possession of a clear and penetrating mind; he is undeniably practical in his fundamental ideas; full of the deepest reverence for all that appears to him beautiful and holy. His style is, as usual, clear, bold, racy. Mr. Ruskin is one of the first writers of the day."—*Economist.*

"The present volume, viewed as a literary achievement, is the highest and most striking evidence of the author's abilities that has yet been published."—*Leader.*

"All, it is to be hoped, will read the book for themselves. They will find it well worth a careful perusal."—*Saturday Review.*

WORKS OF MR. RUSKIN—*continued.*

Modern Painters. Vols. I. and II.

Imp. 8vo. Vol. I., 5th Edit., 18s. cloth. Vol. II., 4th Edit., 10s. 6d. cloth.

"Mr. Ruskin's work will send the painter more than ever to the study of nature; will train men who have always been delighted spectators of nature, to be also attentive observers. Our critics will learn to admire, and mere admirers will learn how to criticise: thus a public will be educated."—*Blackwood's Magazine.*

"A generous and impassioned review of the works of living painters. A hearty and earnest work, full of deep thought, and developing great and striking truths in art."—*British Quarterly Review.*

"A very extraordinary and delightful book, full of truth and goodness, of power and beauty."—*North British Review.*

The Stones of Venice.

Complete in Three Volumes, Imperial 8vo, with Fifty-three Plates and numerous Woodcuts, drawn by the Author. Price 5l. 15s. 6d., cloth.

EACH VOLUME MAY BE HAD SEPARATELY.

Vol. I. THE FOUNDATIONS, *with 21 Plates, price 2l. 2s. 2nd Ed.*

Vol. II. THE SEA STORIES, *with 20 Plates, price 2l. 2s.*

Vol. III. THE FALL, *with 12 Plates, price 1l. 11s. 6d.*

"This book is one which, perhaps, no other man could have written, and one for which the world ought to be and will be thankful. It is in the highest degree eloquent, acute, stimulating to thought, and fertile in suggestion. It will, we are convinced, elevate taste and intellect, raise the tone of moral feeling, kindle benevolence towards men, and increase the love and fear of God."—*Times.*

"The 'Stones of Venice' is the production of an earnest, religious, progressive, and informed mind. The author of this essay on architecture has condensed into it a poetic apprehension, the fruit of awe of God, and delight in nature; a knowledge, love, and just estimate of art; a holding fast to fact and repudiation of hearsay; an historic breadth, and a fearless challenge of existing social problems, whose union we know not where to find paralleled."—*Spectator.*

The Seven Lamps of Architecture.

Second Edition, with Fourteen Plates drawn by the Author. Imperial 8vo. Price 1l. 1s. cloth.

"By the 'Seven Lamps of Architecture,' we understand Mr. Ruskin to mean the seven fundamental and cardinal laws, the observance of and obedience to which are indispensable to the architect, who would deserve the name. The politician, the moralist, the divine, will find in it ample store of instructive matter, as well as the artist. The author of this work belongs to a class of thinkers of whom we have too few amongst us."—*Examiner.*

"Mr. Ruskin's book bears so unmistakeably the marks of keen and accurate observation, of a true and subtle judgment and refined sense of beauty, joined with so much earnestness, so noble a sense of the purposes and business of art, and such a command of rich and glowing language, that it cannot but tell powerfully in producing a more religious view of the uses of architecture, and a deeper insight into its artistic principles."—*Guardian.*

Lectures on Architecture and Painting.

With Fourteen Cuts, drawn by the Author. Second Edition. Crown 8vo Price 8s. 6d. cloth.

"Mr. Ruskin's lectures—eloquent, graphic, and impassioned—exposing and ridiculing some of the vices of our present system of building, and exciting his hearers by strong motives of duty and pleasure to attend to architecture—are very successful."—*Economist.*

"We conceive it to be impossible that any intelligent persons could listen to the lectures, however they might differ from the judgments asserted, and from the general propositions laid down, without an elevating influence and an aroused enthusiasm."—*Spectator.*

RECENT WORKS.

Captivity of Russian Princesses in the Caucasus: including a Seven Months' Residence in Shamil's Seraglio, in the Years 1854-5. Translated from the Russian, by H. S. Edwards.

With an authentic Portrait of Shamil, a Plan of his House, and a Map.
Post 8vo, price 10*s.* 6*d. cloth.*

"A book than which there are few novels more interesting. It is a romance of the Caucasus. The account of life in the house of Shamil is full and very entertaining; and of Shamil himself we see much."—*Examiner.*

"The story is certainly one of the most curious we have read; it contains the best popular notice of the social polity of Shamil and the manners of his people."—*Leader.*

"The narrative is well worth reading."—*Athenæum.*

Esmond. By W. M. Thackeray, Esq.

A New Edition in One Volume, Crown 8vo, price 6s. cloth.

"Apart from its special merits "Esmond" must be read just now as an introduction to "The Virginians." It is quite impossible fully to understand and enjoy the latter story without a good knowledge of "Esmond." The two first numbers of "The Virginians" abound with references which can only be properly appreciated by those who have the previous history of the Esmond family fresh in their recollection. The new tale is in the strictest sense the sequel of the old, not only introducing the same characters, but continuing their history at a later period."—*Leader.*

"Mr. Thackeray has selected for his hero a very noble type of the cavalier softening into the man of the eighteenth century, and for his heroine one of the sweetest women that ever breathed from canvas or from book since Raffaelle painted and Shakspeare wrote. The style is manly, clear, terse, and vigorous, reflecting every mood—pathetic, graphic, or sarcastic—of the writer."—*Spectator.*

The Principles of Agriculture; especially Tropical. By P. Lovell Phillips, M.D.

Demy 8vo, price 7s. 6d. cloth.

"This volume should be in every farmhouse, and it would pay a landlord to present it to his tenants."—*Critic.*

"This treatise contains nearly all that is known of the science of agriculture."—*Observer.*

Religion in Common Life. By William Ellis.

Post 8vo, price 7s. 6d. cloth.

"A book addressed to young people of the upper ten thousand upon social duties. Mr. Ellis has sound views, and his style is simple and clear."—*Examiner.*

"Lessons in Political Economy for young people by a skilful hand; a clear knowledge is imparted, and sensible views are worked out to demonstration. We cordially recommend this work to all who are interested in the education of the young."—*Economist.*

Victoria, and the Australian Gold Mines, in 1857; *with Notes on the Overland Route.* By William Westgarth.

Post 8vo, with Maps, price 10s. 6d., cloth.

"Mr. Westgarth has produced a reliable and readable book well stocked with information, and pleasantly interspersed with incidents of travel and views of colonial life. It is clear, sensible, and suggestive."—*Athenæum.*

"A lively account of the most wonderful bit of colonial experience that the world's history has furnished."—*Examiner.*

"We think Mr. Westgarth's book much the best which has appeared on Australia since the great crisis in its history."—*Saturday Review.*

"A rational, vigorous, illustrative report upon the progress of the greatest colony in Australia."—*Leader.*

"The volume contains a large amount of statistical and practical information relating to Victoria."—*Spectator.*

"To those who refer to these pages for solid and guiding information, they will prove most valuable."—*Globe.*

"The best book on the subject.—*Critic.*

RECENT WORKS—*continued.*

The Life of Charlotte Brontë.

Author of "Jane Eyre," "Shirley," "Villette," &c.
By Mrs. Gaskell, Author of "North and South," &c.

Third Edition, Revised, Two Volumes, Post 8vo, with a Portrait of Miss Brontë and a View of Haworth Church and Parsonage. Price 24s. cloth.

"We regard the record as a monument of courage and endurance, of suffering and triumph. . . . . All the secrets of the literary workmanship of the authoress of 'Jane Eyre' are unfolded in the course of this extraordinary narrative."—*Times.*

"Mrs. Gaskell has produced one of the best biographies of a woman by a woman which we can recall to mind."—*Athenæum.*

"Mrs. Gaskell's 'Life of Charlotte Brontë' has placed her on a level with the best biographers of any country."—*Globe.*

"This work cannot fail to be of the deepest interest; and it has a special interest for female readers."—*Economist.*

"The whole strange and pathetic story of the Brontë family is faithfully told in Mrs. Gaskell's memoir."—*Critic.*

The Sea Officer's Manual; being a Compendium of the Duties of a Commander; First, Second, Third, and Fourth Officer; Officer of the Watch; and Midshipman in the Mercantile Navy. By Captain A. Parish, of the East India Merchant Service.

Second Edition, Small Post 8vo, price 5s. cloth.

"A very lucid and compendious manual. We would recommend youths intent upon a seafaring life to study it."—*Athenæum.*

"A little book that ought to be in great request among young seamen."—*Examiner.*

Third Series of Sermons.

By the late Rev. Fred. W. Robertson, A.M., Incumbent of Trinity Chapel, Brighton.

Second Edition, Post 8vo, with Portrait, price 9s. cloth.

FIRST SERIES—*Fourth Edition, Post 8vo, price 9s. cloth.*

SECOND SERIES—*Fourth Edition, price 9s. cloth.*

"Very beautiful in feeling and occasionally striking and forcible in conception to a remarkable degree."—*Guardian.*

"Mr. Robertson, of Brighton, is a name familiar to most of us, and honoured by all to whom it is familiar."—*Globe.*

"These sermons are full of thought and beauty. There is not a sermon in the series that does not furnish evidence of originality without extravagance, of discrimination without tediousness, and of piety without cant or conventionalism."—*British Quarterly.*

Antiquities of Kertch, and Researches in the Cimmerian Bosphorus. By Duncan McPherson, M.D., of the Madras Army, F.R.G.S., M.A.I., Inspector-General of Hospitals, Turkish Contingent.

Imperial Quarto, with Fourteen Plates and numerous Illustrations, including Eight Coloured Fac-Similes of Relics of Antique Art, price Two Guineas.

"It is a volume which deserves the careful attention of every student of classical antiquity. No one can fail to be pleased with a volume which has so much to attract the eye and to gratify the love of beauty and elegance in design. . . . . The volume is got up with great care and taste, and forms one of the handsomest works that have recently issued from the English Press."—*Saturday Review.*

RECENT WORKS—*continued.*

Annals of British Legislation, a Classified Summary of Parliamentary Papers. Edited by PROFESSOR LEONE LEVI.

THE TWENTY-THIRD PART IS JUST ISSUED.

"A series that, if it be always managed as it is now by Professor Levi, will last as long as there remains a legislature in Great Britain."—*Examiner.*

"It would not be easy to over-estimate the utility of Professor Levi's serial. It has the merit of being an excellent idea zealously carried out."—*Athenæum.*

"We cannot imagine a more truly valuable and nationally important work than this. It is impossible to over-estimate its usefulness."—*Civil Service Gazette.*

Life and Sermons of Tauler.

Translated by MISS SUSANNA WINKWORTH. With a Preface by the REV. CHARLES KINGSLEY.

Small 4to, Printed on Tinted Paper, and bound in antique style, with red edges, suitable for a Present. Price 15s.

A Visit to Salt Lake; being a Journey across the Plains to the Mormon Settlements at Utah. By WILLIAM CHANDLESS.

Post 8vo, with a Map, price 9s. cloth.

The Political Life of Sir Robert Peel.

By THOMAS DOUBLEDAY.

Two Volumes, 8vo, price 18s. cloth.

***The European Revolutions of* 1848.**

By EDWARD CAYLEY.

Crown 8vo, price 6s. cloth.

Signs of the Times; or, The Dangers to Religious Liberty in the Present Day. By the CHEVALIER BUNSEN. Translated by MISS SUSANNA WINKWORTH.

One Volume, 8vo, price 16s. cloth.

Stories and Sketches. By JAMES PAYN.

Post 8vo, price 8s. 6d. cloth.

Stoney's Residence in Tasmania.

Demy 8vo, with Plates, Cuts, and a Map, price 14s. cloth.

The Court of Henry VIII.: being a Selection of the Despatches of SEBASTIAN GIUSTINIAN, *Venetian Ambassador,* 1515-1519. Translated by RAWDON BROWN. *Two Vols., crown 8vo, price 21s. cloth.*

Sight-seeing in Germany and the Tyrol, in the Autumn of 1855. By SIR JOHN FORBES, Author of "A Physician's Holiday," &c.

Post 8vo, with Map and View, price 10s. 6d. cloth.

RECENT WORKS—*continued.*

Conolly on the Treatment of the Insane.
Demy 8vo, price 14s. cloth.

Hopkins's Handbook of Average.
8vo, price 12s. 6d. cloth.

Morice's Hand-Book of British Maritime Law.
8vo, price 5s., cloth.

Adams's History and Topography of the Isle of Wight.
Quarto, 25 Steel Plates, cloth, gilt edges, price 2l. 2s.

Waring's Manual of Therapeutics.
Fcap. 8vo, price 12s. 6d. cloth.

Vogel on Disorders of the Blood.
Translated by CHUNDER COOMAR DEY.
8vo, price 7s. 6d. cloth.

Duncan's Campaign with the Turks in Asia.
Two Vols., post 8vo, price 21s. cloth.

Ross's Account of Red River Settlement.
One Volume, post 8vo, price 10s. 6d. cloth.

Ross's Fur Hunters of the Far West.
Two Volumes, post 8vo. With Map and Plate. 21s. cloth.

Russo-Turkish Campaigns of 1828-9.
By COLONEL CHESNEY, R.A., D.C.L., F.R.S.
Third Edition. Post 8vo, with Maps, price 12s. cloth.

Thomson's Military Forces and Institutions of Great Britain.
8vo, price 15s. cloth.

The Militiaman at Home and Abroad; being the History of a Militia Regiment.
With Two Etchings, by JOHN LEECH. *Post 8vo, price 9s. cloth.*

Levi's Manual of the Mercantile Law of Great Britain and Ireland.
8vo, price 12s. cloth.

Thomson's Laws of War Affecting Commerce and Shipping.
Second Edition, greatly enlarged. 8vo, price 4s. 6d. boards.

WORKS ON INDIA AND THE EAST.

The Commerce of India with Europe, and its Political Effects. By B. A. Irving, Esq., Author of "The Theory and Practice of Caste."
Post 8vo, price 7s. 6d. cloth.

Views and Opinions of Brigadier-General Jacob, C.B. Collected and Edited by Captain Lewis Pelly, Late Political Secretary Persian Expeditionary Force. *Demy 8vo, price 12s. cloth.*

Papers of the late Lord Metcalfe. Selected and Edited by J. W. Kaye.
Demy 8vo, price 16s. cloth.

The Life of Mahomet and History of Islam to the Era of the Hegira. By William Muir, Esq., Bengal Civil Service.
Two Volumes 8vo, price 32s. cloth.

Tracts on the Native Army of India. By Brigadier-General Jacob, C.B.
8vo, price 2s. 6d.

Rifle Practice. By Brigadier-General Jacob, C.B.
Fourth Edition, 8vo, price 2s.

The English in Western India; being the Early History of the Factory at Surat, of Bombay. By Philip Anderson, A.M.
Second Edition, 8vo, price 14s. cloth.

Life in Ancient India. By Mrs. Speir.
With Sixty Illustrations by G. Scharf. *8vo, price 15s., elegantly bound in cloth, gilt edges.*

The Cauvery, Kistnah, and Godavery: being a Report on the Works constructed on those Rivers, for the Irrigation of Provinces in the Presidency of Madras. By R. Baird Smith, F.G.S., Lt.-Col. Bengal Engineers, &c., &c.
In demy 8vo, with 19 Plans, price 28s. cloth.

The Bhilsa Topes; or, Buddhist Monuments of Central India. By Major Cunningham.
One Volume, 8vo, with Thirty-three Plates, price 30s. cloth.

The Chinese and their Rebellions. By Thomas Taylor Meadows.
One Thick Volume, 8vo, with Maps, price 18s. cloth.

WORKS ON INDIA AND THE EAST—*continued.*

On the Culture and Commerce of Cotton in India. By Dr. FORBES ROYLE. 8vo, *price* 18*s.* *cloth.*

Review of the Measures adopted in India for the Improved Culture of Cotton. By Dr. FORBES ROYLE. 8vo, 2*s.* 6*d.* *cloth.*

The Fibrous Plants of India fitted for Cordage, Clothing, and Paper. By Dr. FORBES ROYLE. 8vo, *price* 12*s.* *cloth.*

The Productive Resources of India. By Dr. FORBES ROYLE. Super Royal 8vo, price 14*s.* cloth.

A Sketch of Assam; with some Account of the Hill Tribes. Coloured Plates, 8vo, price 14*s.* cloth.

Butler's Travels and Adventures in Assam. One Volume 8vo, with Plates, price 12*s.* cloth.

Dr. Wilson on Infanticide in Western India. Demy 8vo, price 12*s.*

Rev. James Coley's Journal of the Sutlej Campaign. Fcap. 8vo, price 4*s.* cloth.

Crawfurd's Grammar and Dictionary of the Malay Language. 2 vols. 8vo, price 36*s.* cloth.

Roberts's Indian Exchange Tables. 8vo. Second Edition, enlarged, price 10*s.* 6*d.* cloth.

Waring on Abscess in the Liver. 8vo, price 3*s.* 6*d.*

Laurie's Second Burmese War—Rangoon. Post 8vo, with Plates, price 10*s.* 6*d.* cloth.

Laurie's Pegu. Post 8vo, price 14*s.* cloth.

Boyd's Turkish Interpreter: a Grammar of the Turkish Language. 8vo, price 12*s.*

Bridgnell's Indian Commercial Tables. Royal 8vo, price 21*s.*, half-bound.

The Bombay Quarterly Review. Nos. 1 to 9 at 5*s.* 10 and 12, price 6*s.* each.

Baillie's Land Tax of India. According to the Moohummudan Law. 8vo, price 6*s.* cloth.

Baillie's Moohummudan Law of Sale. 8vo, price 14*s.* cloth.

Irving's Theory and Practice of Caste. 8vo, price 5*s.* cloth.

Gingell's Ceremonial Usages of the Chinese. Imperial 8vo, price 9*s.* cloth.

NEW CHEAP SERIES OF POPULAR WORKS.

In Small Post 8vo, with large Type, on good Paper, and neat cloth binding.

Lectures on the English Humourists of the 18th Century. By W. M. Thackeray, Author of "Vanity Fair," "The Virginians," &c. *Price 2s. 6d. cloth.*

British Rule in India. By Harriet Martineau. *Price 2s. 6d., cloth.*

The Political Economy of Art. By John Ruskin, M.A. *Price 2s. 6d. cloth.*

TO BE FOLLOWED BY

The Town; its Memorable Characters and Events. By Leigh Hunt. *With 45 Cuts.*

AND OTHER STANDARD WORKS.

CHEAP SERIES OF POPULAR FICTIONS.

Well printed, in large type, on good paper, and strongly bound in cloth.

Jane Eyre. By Currer Bell. *Price 2s. 6d. cloth.*

"'Jane Eyre' is a remarkable production. Freshness and originality, truth and passion, singular felicity in the description of natural scenery, and in the analysation of human thought, enable this tale to stand boldly out from the mass, and to assume its own place in the bright field of romantic literature."—*Times.*

Shirley. By Currer Bell. *Price 2s. 6d. cloth.*

"The peculiar power which was so greatly admired in 'Jane Eyre' is not absent from this book. It possesses deep interest, and an irresistible grasp of reality. There are scenes which, for strength and delicacy of emotion, are not transcended in the range of English fiction."—*Examiner.*

Villette. By Currer Bell. *Price 2s. 6d. cloth.*

"This novel amply sustains the fame of the author of 'Jane Eyre' and 'Shirley' as an original and powerful writer."—*Examiner.*

Wuthering Heights and Agnes Grey. By Ellis and Acton Bell. With Memoir by Currer Bell. *Price 2s. 6d. cloth.*

A Lost Love. By Ashford Owen. *Price 2s. cloth.* (*Now Ready.*)

TO BE FOLLOWED BY

Deerbrook. By Harriet Martineau.

School for Fathers. By Talbot Gwynne.

Paul Ferroll. Fourth Edition.

NEW NOVELS.

(TO BE HAD AT ALL LIBRARIES).

Maud Skillicorne's Penance. By MARY CATHERINE JACKSON, Author of "The Story of My Wardship." 2 vols.

"The style is natural, and displays considerable dramatic power."—*Critic.*

The Cruelest Wrong of All. By the Author of "Margaret; or, Prejudice at Home." 1 vol.

"It has the first requisite of a work of fiction—it is amusing."—*Globe.*

The Moors and the Fens. By F. G. TRAFFORD. 3 vols.

"The plot is unhackneyed, and the composition is particularly good."—*Critic.*

"The plot is natural, and skilfully worked out; many of the scenes are described with great power, and the characters look like portraits from life."—*Ladies' Newspaper.*

Gaston Bligh. By L. S. LAVENU, Author of "Erlesmere." 2 vols.

"'Gaston Bligh' is a good story, admirably told, full of stirring incident, and abounding in clever sketches of character."—*Critic.*

"A charming work of fiction."—*Morning Chronicle.*

"The story is told with great power; the whole book sparkles with *esprit.*"—*Press.*

The Three Chances. By the Author of "The Fair Carew." 3 vols.

"The authoress has a mind that thoroughly appreciates the humorous in life and character."—*Globe.*

"This novel is full of good sense, good thought, and good writing."—*Statesman.*

The White House by the Sea: a Love Story. By M. BETHAM-EDWARDS. 2 vols.

Riverston. By GEORGIANA M. CRAIK. 3 vols.

The Professor. By CURRER BELL. 2 vols.

The Noble Traytour. A Chronicle. 3 vols.

Farina; a Legend of Cologne. By GEORGE MEREDITH. 1 vol.

Below the Surface: a Story of English Country Life. 3 vols.

The Roua Pass; or, Englishmen in the Highlands. By ERICK MACKENZIE. 3 vols.

Kathie Brande. By HOLME LEE. 2 vols.

Friends of Bohemia; or, Phases of London Life. By E. M. WHITTY, Author of "The Governing Classes." 2 vols.

Lucian Playfair. By THOMAS MACKERN. 3 vols.

NOVELS FORTHCOMING.

Sylvan Holt's Daughter. By HOLME LEE, Author of "Kathie Brande," &c. 3 vols.

Lost and Won. By GEORGIANA M. CRAIK, Author of "Riverston." 1 vol.

My Lady. 2 vols.

An Old Debt. By FLORENCE DAWSON. 2 vols.

Mutation. 3 vols.

Old and Young. 1 vol.

NEW BOOKS FOR YOUNG READERS.

By the Author of "Round the Fire," &c.

Old Gingerbread and the School-boys.
With Four Coloured Plates. (*Nearly Ready.*)

Unica: a Story for Sunday.
With Four Cuts. (*Nearly Ready.*)

Uncle Jack, the Fault Killer.
With Four Illustrations. Price 3s. cloth.

"An excellent little book of moral improvement made pleasant to children; it is far beyond the common-place moral tale in design and execution."—*Globe.*

Willie's Birthday; showing how a Little Boy did what he Liked, and how he Enjoyed it.
With Four Illustrations. Price 2s. 6d., cloth

Willie's Rest: a Sunday Story.
With Four Illustrations. Price 2s. 6d. cloth.

"Graceful little tales, containing some pretty parables, and a good deal of simple fooling."—*Economist.*

"Extremely well written story books, amusing and moral, and got up in a very handsome style."—*Morning Herald.*

Round the Fire: Six Stories for Young Readers.
Square 16mo, with Four Illustrations, price 3s. cloth.

"Charmingly written tales for the young."—*Leader.*

"Six delightful little stories."—*Guardian.*

"Simple and very interesting."—*National Review.*

"True children's stories."—*Athenæum.*

The King of the Golden River; or, the Black Brothers. By JOHN RUSKIN, M.A.
Third Edition, with 22 Illustrations by RICHARD DOYLE. *Price 2s. 6d.*

This little fancy tale is by a master-hand. The story has a charming moral."—*Examiner.*

MISCELLANEOUS.

Elementary Works on Social Economy. Uniform in foolscap 8vo, half-bound.

I.—OUTLINES OF SOCIAL ECONOMY. 1*s.* 6*d.*

II.—PROGRESSIVE LESSONS IN SOCIAL SCIENCE.

III.—INTRODUCTION TO THE SOCIAL SCIENCES. 2*s.*

IV.—OUTLINES OF THE UNDERSTANDING. 2*s.*

V.—WHAT AM I? WHERE AM I? WHAT OUGHT I TO DO? &c. 1*s.* sewed.

Swainson's Lectures on New Zealand. Crown 8vo, price 2*s.* 6*d.* cloth.

Swainson's Account of Auckland. Post 8vo, with a View, price 6*s.* cloth.

Playford's Hints for Investing Money. Second Edition, post 8vo, price 2*s.* 6*d.* cloth.

Sir John Forbes's Memorandums in Ireland. Two Vols., post 8vo, price 1*l.* 1*s.* cloth.

Leigh Hunt's Men, Women, and Books. Two Vols. Price 10*s.* cloth.

——— *Table Talk.* 3*s.* 6*d.* cloth.

——— *Wit and Humour.* 5*s.* cloth.

——— *Jar of Honey.* 5*s.* cloth.

Sir John Herschel's Astronomical Observations made at the Cape of Good Hope. 4to, with plates, price 4*l.* 4*s.* cloth.

Darwin's Geological Observations on Coral Reefs, Volcanic Islands, and on South America. With maps, plates, and woodcuts, 10*s.* 6*d.* cloth.

Levi's Commercial Law of the World. Two Vols., royal 4to, price 6*l.* cloth.

Juvenile Delinquency. By M. HILL and C. F. CORNWALLIS. Post 8vo, price 6*s.* cloth.

Doubleday's True Law of Population. Third Edition, 8vo, 10*s.* cloth.

McCann's Argentine Provinces, &c. Two Vols., post 8vo, with illustrations, price 24*s.* cloth.

Rowcroft's Tales of the Colonies. Sixth Edit. 6*s.* cloth.

Goethe's Conversations with Eckermann. Translated by JOHN OXENFORD. Two Vols., post 8vo, 10*s.* cloth.

Kavanagh's Women of Christianity Exemplary for Piety and Charity. Post 8vo, with Portraits, price 12*s.*, in embossed cloth, gilt edges.

POETRY.

The Six Legends of King Goldenstar. By the late ANNA BRADSTREET. Fcap. 8vo, price 5*s.*

"The author evinces more than ordinary power, a vivid imagination, guided by a mind of lofty aim."—*Globe.*

England in Time of War. By SYDNEY DOBELL, Author of "Balder," "The Roman," &c. Crown 8vo, 5*s.* cloth.

"That Mr. Dobell is a poet, 'England in time of War' bears witness in many single lines, and in two or three short poems."—*Athenæum.*

The Cruel Sister, AND OTHER POEMS. Fcap. 8vo, 4*s.* cl.

"There are traces of power, and the versification displays freedom and skill."—*Guardian.*

Poems of Past Years. By SIR ARTHUR HALLAM ELTON, Bart., M.P. Fcap. 8vo, 3*s.* cloth.

"A refined, scholarly, and gentlemanly mind is apparent all through this volume."—*Leader.*

Poems. By MRS. FRANK P. FELLOWS. Fcap. 8vo, 3*s.* cl.

"There is easy simplicity in the diction, and elegant naturalness in the thought."—*Spectator.*

Lota, AND OTHER POEMS. By DEVON HARRIS. Fcap. 8vo, 4*s.* cloth.

"Displaying high poetic genius and power."—*Eclectic Review.*

Poetry from Life. By C. M. K. Fcap. 8vo, cl. gilt, 5*s.*

"Elegant verses. The author has a pleasing fancy and a refined mind."—*Economist.*

Poems. By WALTER R. CASSELS. Fcap. 8vo, price 3*s.* 6*d.* cloth.

"Mr. Cassels has deep poetical feeling, and gives promise of real excellence. His poems are written sometimes with a strength of expression by no means common."—*Guardian.*

Garlands of Verse. By THOMAS LEIGH. Fcap. 8vo, price 5*s.* cloth.

"One of the best things in the 'Garlands of Verse' is an Ode to Toil. There, as elsewhere, there is excellent feeling."—*Examiner.*

Balder. By SYDNEY DOBELL. Crown 8vo, 7*s.* 6*d.* cloth.

"The writer has fine qualities; his level of thought is lofty, and his passion for the beautiful has the truth of instinct."—*Athenæum.*

Poems. By WILLIAM BELL SCOTT. Fcap. 8vo, 5*s.* cl.

"Mr. Scott has poetical feeling, keen observation, deep thought, and command of language."—*Spectator.*

Poems. By MARY MAYNARD. Fcap. 8vo, 4*s.* cloth.

"We have rarely met with a volume of poems displaying so large an amount of power, blended with so much delicacy of feeling and grace of expression."—*Church of England Quarterly.*

Poems. By CURRER, ELLIS, and ACTON BELL. Fcap. 8vo, 4*s.* cloth.

Select Odes of Horace. In English Lyrics. By J. T. BLACK. Fcap. 8vo, price 4*s.* cloth.

"Rendered into English Lyrics with a vigour and heartiness rarely, if ever, surpassed."—*Critic.*

London: Printed by SMITH, ELDER & CO., Little Green Arbour Court.